THE ROOTS
OF
READING

Insights on Speech Acquisition and Reading

DR. IJYA C. TULLOSS

authorHOUSE®

AuthorHouse™
1663 Liberty Drive
Bloomington, IN 47403
www.authorhouse.com
Phone: 1 (800) 839-8640

Published by AuthorHouse 03/07/2019

ISBN: 978-1-5462-7536-7 (sc)
ISBN: 978-1-5462-7535-0 (hc)
ISBN: 978-1-5462-7537-4 (e)

Library of Congress Control Number: 2019900286

DEDICATION

This book is dedicated to my two sons, Mark and Carlos Tulloss whose love of learning inspired me to be an educator and a writer.

Mom

TABLE OF CONTENTS

ABOUT THE AUTHOR

I trained as a chemist, earned my MS. in Chemistry at Northwestern University and worked for Abbott Laboratories. With the birth of my first son, my interest shifted to education. I became a certified Montessori teacher in Early Childhood and Elementary Education. After the birth of my second son, nine years later, I founded my own Montessori school, Glencoe Montessori School. I became a certified K-9 elementary teacher in the State of Illinois, earned my doctorate in Early and Middle Childhood Education from Nova Southeastern University.

Coming from a scientific background and entering into a new field of endeavor, I purposely sought out activities that enriched my background in the humanities. These new activities gave me a more balanced background to go into teaching. I engaged in International folk dancing for 10 years, ballroom dancing for 14 years, Two-step dancing, for two years. I sang in the church choir for 12 years and sang in women's barbershop chorus for a year. I rejoined the barbershop chorus five years ago and am currently engaged in singing with the group. Meanwhile I was convinced that communication through speech was an asset so I joined Toastmaster International, a public speaking club.

Following my mother's suggestion to continue studying all throughout life, I picked up courses here and there on cultural anthropology, Adlerian psychology, Theosophy, Kabbalah, and spirituality. My mother's last suggestion was, "If you run out of things to study, take up law." I have not embarked on the study of law as yet. Give me some time.

The varied experiences and training have broadened my worldview and enriched my pool of resources to address life's vicissitudes. I have become passionate in the area of reading and writing. Nothing compares to the joy of witnessing a child reading a whole book all by himself for the first time. Indeed teaching a child to write and read is a gift that opens doors to learning about himself, the world we live in and the people and inhabitants therein.

This book is my gift to all learners so that all may read. Join me in this endeavor.

FOREWORD

This book is about learning to read and write or learning to write and read.

A parent, a teacher or a mentor will find this book easy to use and easy to follow with its step-by-step narrative.

With a science background working with test tubes for eight years and now thrown into a Montessori classroom with three-, four-, and five-year olds, I was at a loss on what to do and what I can contribute to the field. Little by little I felt at home in Montessori education. Instead of just washing the "line" as the taped floor was called, I taught the children to wash the 'perimeter' of the square or the 'circumference' of the circle or the 'area' of the square. I used 'petals' for the sweeping exercise. That was more environmentally correct since I felt bad about playing with rice which we eat.

I learned to sing 'Over the River and through the Woods' for Thanksgiving and 'Here Comes Peter Cottontail' for Easter. I was comfortable with music and dancing. My internship supervisor showed Hungarian dance steps. That perked me up and from that time on I no longer felt like a stranger in that room. I taught the children to sing 'Bahay Kubo,' a Philippine song about my little nipa hut surrounded by various vegetables. To my surprise, the children did not resist learning a song in another language. I felt good that I could teach children and the classroom experience was enjoyable.

I was fascinated with building as many variations as I could make with the red rods. After building the staircase from the shortest to the longest rod, I explored designs that could be made. I could make triangles, rhombi, a sunburst or a maze. I made a fabric box of matching squares for designs such as stripes, polka dot, printed design or plain.

I was looking forward to teaching them language and math. That did not happen during my internship year. The following year, I was the lead teacher of my own class. There was one problem. My assistant became ill and had to quit her job. She was not replaced so I had to work by myself with fourteen children. I could not find time to sit down one-on-one to teach the alphabet with sandpaper letters.

From the lectures at the training program, I learned that children are hungry for words and are sensitive to words at this age. I engaged children in conversations to discuss stories we read. Michael enlightened me with his vocabulary. I told the story about the Seven Chinese Brothers. One brother committed a crime. It was not serious. He was guilty of something that was not too serious. Michael interjected that it was a **misdemeanor**. Michael's mother was a lawyer. Michael was only four years old.

Pam's mother reported that her daughter exclaimed that she was wearing stripes. New vocabulary was evident.

To dismiss the class at the end of the day, I flashed one by one a card bearing child's printed name as I sounded out the first letter followed by the rest of the sounds. I was surprised that such a simple activity meant so much to the class. Parents were excited in telling me that their children were naming the letters at home – K for Karen, A for Amanda etc.

I needed someone to help me with teaching the sounds of the alphabet. I approached the director. My idea was to train volunteers who then could come once a week to help. She thought that mothers from the other classrooms would be interested too. We went ahead with our plan, conducted a training session and had a few volunteers trained to help teach the sounds of the alphabet.

Many things happened during the year. Everyone learned something:
The mothers learned the sounds of the letters. This was new to them and they admitted that they would not have learned to say the sounds had they not come to the workshop.

The children learned to sound out the letters. Some picked out a few while others learned to sound out almost all of the letters of the alphabet. Since there was no pressure in the process, I figured out that we would continue with the lessons in the same manner the following year.

I learned about motivation. Some children could not wait until they had their lessons at the 'sound' table. Some were not interested in learning the sounds of letters, others came to honor the invitation to join the teacher at the table.

While we were still in the stage of learning the sounds of the letters, I was thinking ahead, sounding out letters to spell words with short vowels. My brain was scanning the room for objects that spell short vowel words. I was inspired to search for words in the stories we read, in the songs we sang and in the poems we recited.

Learning was fun to all concerned.

Where do we go from here? We were still a long way from being able to read books. Simply knowing short vowels was not helpful enough in decoding words found in books. Jason and Carlos, my son, were constantly asking what this word or that word says as we passed by signs along the street.

I then introduced long vowels.

Long vowels:

> **ee** as in **ee**l or gr**ee**n
> **oo** as in m**oo**n
> **ai** as in **ai**m or s**ai**l
> **ie** as in p**ie**
> **oa** as in **oa**k or g**oa**t
> **ue** as in bl**ue**

The number of words Jason and Carlos could read increased tremendously. I then introduced consonant digraphs.

Consonant digraphs:

> **ch** as in chip
> **sh** as in ship
> **th** as in thick   **th** as in then
> **wh** as in when
> final **ng** as in king final   **nk** as in pink.

At this point we discovered that the commercially available set of sandpaper letters does not contain **ng** and **nk.** We had to make them out of cardboard.

Then one day, Jason could read a whole book all by himself. I was pleased with his achievement and wondered if Carlos would soon follow Jason's footsteps.

One afternoon, I sent Carlos to a babysitter, a mother of one of the teachers. When we picked him up, the babysitter asked if we noticed that Carlos could read a book by himself. She said Carlos could read all the children's books on their bookshelf. I was so excited at the news we drove home in a hurry.

When we got home, I picked a book at random from the shelf and asked Carlos to read it. Carlos read the book with no trouble. We picked another book and again, Carlos read it fluently. My husband handed him a copy of National Geographic and Carlos could read the article. The interesting thing was that he would pause to ask what the word meant after he just decoded what it said. That was so exhilarating for the family to watch!

We knew then that the system works. Everybody can learn to read and write. We need to teach them the sounds of a few letters at a time while we continue to read stories to them every day. We also need to sound out words and blend the sounds to say the word.

Why do we write?

Writing enables us to record events, agreements, transactions as well as our private thoughts and feelings. When we write, it is like taking a snap shot of how we feel at the moment. We can revisit this feeling when we read the diary or journal at a later date.

Whereas oral communication requires the speaker to be within ear-shot distance to the listener at the same time, writing can be transmitted across time and space. Through writing, the knowledge of one generation could be passed to the next. Without such means, valuable information and wisdom could be lost.

From a practical sense, writing allows us to quickly jot down information on paper instead of relying solely on our memory. The written notes help us recall what we wrote. What is forgotten mentally could be irretrievably lost.

Writing is all around us. Whether it is reading signs, directions or contracts, we need to read accurately or experience negative consequences.

To fully participate in our technologically advanced society, one has to be sufficiently literate to read and write to function.

Through writing, we can learn about history, culture, science, geography and subjects of personal interest.

Amidst the need for a high degree of literacy, we continue to see children unable to read beyond the third grade level, students dropping out of high school when they find themselves unable to keep up with school work.

Grown-ups unable to read proficiently deprive themselves of better paying jobs. They look as though they could read when in fact they are only pretending to read.

We have successfully sent men to the moon and back yet we remain unsuccessful in addressing the reading problem of our population.

Why is instruction needed to read and write?

The amazing feat of speech acquisition exhibited by the child with hardly any formal lesson on language gives us the impression that reading can be learned with the same ease. All we need to do is read to the child every day and he learns to read with no further instruction. Such is **not** the case with reading and writing.

While we, humans, are wired to learn to speak the language that we hear, we are not so wired for reading and writing. (13) We have the capacity to learn to read and write but we have to have instruction to develop such skills.

The answer to the above question lies in evolutionary biology.

Charles Darwin and the finches

When Charles Darwin as a young naturalist travelled with the H.M.S. Beagle on a voyage of discovery to the Galapagos Islands, (6) he collected a good number of specimen. As a taxidermist, he was able to preserve the specimens and brought them back to England. He thought he collected all kinds of finches. He turned these over to the ornithologist for closer scrutiny.

Darwin was surprised to hear that each different-looking bird was of a different species. He was first intrigued how the finches that originated from South America and somehow ended in the Galapagos Islands no longer look identical to their ancestors. In fact different birds from different islands isolated from one another looked differently from one another.

It was only through the process of evolution that one can explain this phenomenon. At the time of Darwin, the prevailing idea was creationism, each species was created in its final form at the time of creation and no further change took place among the species over time.

With evolution, an organism adapts to its environment, changing slowly over time in order to survive. (6) Thus, the following adaptations can be seen in the present-day forms of the finches:

Some developed strong bills for crushing seeds. Some developed long slender beaks adapted for eating insects. Others developed special adaptation for collecting nectar from plants. Each species adapted to its niche in order to meet its basic need for food.

Evolution

According to Charles Darwin, organisms adapt to their environment to address stressors and other challenges in order to survive. The process of adaptation consists of making small changes with their biological structure and/or metabolic processes over a long period of time. This change is called **evolution.**

Parallels to Human Evolution

The same general principle can be seen with human evolution. When humans evolved from walking on fours like a dog to standing on two feet and walking bipedal, (10) we freed up our hands for use with tools instead of supporting the body while crawling on all fours. (20) (21) Standing on two feet made us appear taller which helped scare the animals.

Learning to talk gave rise to oral communication, a more precise and faster way of communicating what we mean compared to the use of pantomimes, gestures and hand signals. We continue to communicate verbally. We do not need to be taught to walk nor talk, physical maturation is all that is needed. (3) A child walks at around 12 -18 months; talks at around 18-30 months. These skills are wired into our genes.

We have only been writing for 5000 years. (22) This claim is based on the earliest Egyptian writing records. Scientists think that it takes about 10,000 years to incorporate a behavioral trait into our genes. It is therefore too early to incorporate reading-writing behavioral traits into our genes. Unlike walking and talking which only require physical maturation for the individual to start walking or talking, we have to be taught how to read and write.

To put it more simply, we have not evolved to the point where the ability to read and write becomes a part of our genetic make-up. If it were so, reading and writing would be as natural as walking and talking. (13)

THE NATURE OF LANGUAGE

HOW CHILDREN ACQUIRE SPEECH

An infant is not born speaking. One has to acquire speech. However, in a relatively short time, a four-year-old, learns to speak with correct grammar using a wide range of vocabulary. In short, the child learned to speak like a native speaker without formal lessons on language. Comparing this feat to an adult learner, the child's accomplishment is amazing.

We marvel at how an infant acquires the speech that one hears in a very short time with no formal instruction. Only two things are needed: 1) the infant hears people talking to each other (11) and 2) the infant is spoken to.

Language learning is an interactive process with the primary caregiver, the mother in most cases. Watching others speak with each other enhances speech acquisition. It is generally observed that a child learns to speak the language that one hears.

On the second factor, mothers, fathers and other caregivers have intuitively found a way to converse with an infant. The mother speaks slowly in a high-pitched voice. The pronunciation of words is exaggerated. Vowels are formed with special care. Eye contact is maintained while engaging in these conversations. Utterances are short, punctuated with smiles and pleasant facial expressions. The tone of voice is varied to keep infant's attention. Words are repeated several times.

Since the type of speech described above is directed to the infant this has been called **Infant Directed Speech.** (1) Since it is usually the mother who engages in this type of talk it is also called "**motherese.**" Not to leave fathers out, we also call this type of speech "**parentese.**"

> **Infant Directed Speech** (1) may be characterized as:
> slow
> high-pitched
> face-to-face contact with infant
> full attention while speaking
> exaggerated pronunciation of vowels
> few words in an utterance

Although the infant is not talking, he is 'thinking' with images, not with words, while listening and formulating what he would say once he is able to talk. (12) (13)

A give and take in the conversation takes place allowing the infant to "speak" and to listen. This is a lesson on turn-taking. A pleasant, happy visit is enjoyed by both mother and child.

Rapid Development in Speech Acquisition

It is now common knowledge that children's development during the first six years of their life takes place at an unprecedented pace. It is as though we scatter some grass seeds on the yard and in a few days, the seeds have sprung up and we have a green lawn. All we did was to water the lawn and the grass seeds developed spontaneously. The plan for development was inherent in the seeds. We could not make the grass grow, we could only facilitate its growth by providing what the seeds need – soil, water, fertilizer.

The same is true with speech acquisition. We facilitate development of speech but it is the infant who works at listening and making sense of what he hears, trying to produce speech sounds and finally learns to talk like the adults caring for him.

The CDC (3) and other research bodies have compiled developmental landmarks for the purpose of alerting parents that speech therapy may be required. The earlier help is given the better off one could be.

We look at these developmental milestones as general guidelines for conferring with your pediatrician not as absolute yardsticks for comparing your child with the next door neighbor. We accept the fact that individuals differ in their development. A range of behavior or traits could be considered normal. We do not teach the child to speak, we speak to the child. The child is listening intently while we speak.

It is inherent in the child's development to speak at a certain timetable. We facilitate the process of speech development by providing what the child needs. It is advisable to speak to the child as we feed him, dress him or show him different places in the community. The child needs these words as he builds his private dictionary in his brain (18).

STAGES OF DEVELOPMENT IN SPEECH ACQUISITION (3) AND SUGGESTED CAREGIVER SUPPORT ACTIVITIES

Speech acquisition occurs in stages. Supporting development at every stage is important. The following section traces speech development along with suggested activities to support growth and development. We closely observe what the child does, what interests him so we can meet his needs accordingly in a language-enriched environment.

1. Cooing and babbling

The infant coos and babbles to himself. This could be an exercise in voice production, in producing vowels and beginning consonants.

vowel sounds: "oo," "ah," "eh"
consonants: "d," "t," "p." "m."

How an Infant Learns to Call Mama and Papa

At first, the infant could only coo and babble saying "oo," "ee," "ah." He then tries saying consonants like "m," "p," "d," and "t."

To say "m" all he has to do is to close his lips and push some air to make the sound of "m." Pairing "m" with the vowel "ah" one hears the sound of "mah" which we interpret as the sound for calling his mother, "mama".

Making the "p" sound, he first closes his lips then quickly pops the air out between the lips as he says "p." Pairing "p" with the vowel "ah" he says "pah." We interpret the sound "pah" as similar to calling his father, "pa."

To make the "d" sound, he places his tongue on the middle of the front palate and clicks it as he makes the sound of "d." When he pairs the consonant with the vowel, "ah" it sounds like "dah." We interpret the sound as like the sound of calling his father, "dad."

To make the "t" sound, he places his tongue on the front palate and clicks it to say "t." He pairs the consonant "t" with the vowel "ah" and says "tah." We interpret the sound as similar to the first syllable in calling "tatay" which means father in Filipino language.

Caregiver echoes infant's attempt to pronounce consonants and say dada, papa, mama, tata back to the infant.

As we can see, "m," "p," "d," and "t" are the simplest and easiest sounds for the infant to produce. We interpret the resulting utterances of "mama," "papa," "dada," and "tata," as the infant's first endearing calls to his mother and father.

The infant turns his head to direction of sound.

Also at this stage, the infant learns taking turns in conversation. Although the infant does not say anything intelligible to adults, we respond respectfully so infant learns turn-taking in conversations.

We play naming body parts:
"Show me beautiful eyes." Infant blinks eyes.
"Where are your hands? Toes? Fingers?" Infant points at named body part.
We continue to name objects, describe what we are doing, read books to infant, bring child to see neighborhood, give child opportunity to watch others speak to each other. These activities help infant gain a wide vocabulary as he is sensitized to learning words at a record speed.

5

Reading books to children daily expands vocabulary, builds bonding between infant and caregiver and exposes one to vocal variety in reading phrases.

2. One word at a time. (3)

At 18 months, the toddler speaks one's first intelligible words. He speaks one word at a time. The one word spoken stands for a whole sentence. We complete the sentence to the best we can. Toddler says "milk." *We say "You want some milk." "I'll get you some milk."*

Generally we only pay particular attention when the infant speaks his first intelligible words. We secretly hope for the day when the toddler can put sentences together.

3. Infant forms phrases and sentences

At 2 years, child puts two or three words together to form a phrase. We continue adding a word or two to complete the sentence or show understanding of his message. Suddenly, we notice the toddler speaking complete sentences **non-stop** using correct grammar. We wish he would stop.

We continue to read books, sing songs, recite poems to the child.

Child's speech shows use of adjectives, adverbs and prepositions. He asks questions and expects answers.

We try to speak with modifiers in our speech:

*Bring me the **blue** ball.*	(use adjectives to describe noun)
*Talk **quietly.***	(adverb)
*Put the book back **on** the shelf.*	(preposition)

4. Speaks with complete sentences

At 3, he speaks with complete sentences using correct grammar.

5. One seemingly uses incorrect grammar.

Word form previously spoken correctly is used incorrectly due to over generalization of grammar rules deduced by learner. I observed the following "invented" word forms in the toddler's speech.

"I ***putted*** an apple in your lunch box."

(Generalized application of the rule that verbs form past tense by adding **ed** to the infinitive).

"The bird ***builded*** *its nest.*" (The bird built its nest.)

(Some verbs are irregular. They form past tense by a change in form.)

6. Corrects faulty deduction of grammar form of words

At 5, one corrects error due to over generalization of grammar rules and speaks correctly once again.

What is the child doing while observing the people around him?

He is developing concepts about himself, about others and about the world around him.

He is observing that labels are attached to concepts that he had formed.

He is checking out the rules that govern the physical world, the social world and the world of language.

He is formulating what he would say once he can talk. Let's talk about the world of language.

The World of Language

Utterances heard from others have meanings. These utterances which we call words are labels for things or concepts. (4) (17) (18)

Nouns are Names

Things have **names.**

There are apples, oranges and bananas. There are also labels for **categories,** so apples, oranges and bananas are **fruits.** We **eat** apples, oranges and bananas. Things that we eat are called **food.** When we can speak and we know what things are called, we can ask for what we want to eat. We can specify the object that we want.

Prior to being able to speak, we could only point at an object while making some unintelligible sound. It is a trial and error game between the infant and the caregiver. An infant points at an object while making some sounds. The caregiver gives what she thinks the infant wants. It is rejected. A second attempt is made. The infant rejects it too. This continues until the desired object is given. This could be frustrating to the infant. With the aid of speech, one can specify what one wants and minimize the frustration of engaging in a guessing game.

There are **names for singular objects and another name for multiple objects.** Thus we can ask for **one apple** or ask for **two or more apples.**

Words that describe objects

We can specify the apple we want by its color. We can ask for the **red apple** or the **green apple.** Names of objects are called **nouns.** The word 'apple' is a noun. A word that describes, modifies or specifies the noun is called '**an adjective.**' 'Red' and 'green' are examples of adjectives. A noun with its modifier is called a '**noun phrase.**' Some examples of noun phrases are 'a red apple' and 'a green apple.'

Aside from food, we also need clothes. There are shirts and pants to wear. They come in colors. I **wear** my **blue** shirt with my **blue** pants; green shirt with my **green** pants; **brown** shirt with my **brown** pants. We dress according to the weather. On **cool** days we wear a sweater. On **rainy** days we wear a raincoat. In the winter, when it is **cold**, we wear a **warm** coat.

Words that describe a noun are called adjectives. **Blue, green, brown are adjectives**. They describe the clothes we wear. **Cool, rainy and cold** are adjectives describing the kind of weather we have. **Warm** is also an adjective describing the coat to wear in winter.

We can have new **noun phrases** on clothes we wear: 'a blue shirt,' a green shirt' are some examples.

Verbs are action words

My mom **bathes** me to keep me clean. I **play** with my rubber ducky while **taking** a bath. After my bath, my mom **sings** me to sleep. I **sleep** soundly.

Action words are called **verbs. Eat, wear, bathes, play, taking, sings, sleep** are examples of **verbs**. A word that modifies a verb is called an

adverb. A verb along with its modifiers is called a **verb phrase**. 'Sleep soundly' is a verb phrase.

Strings of words may or may not have a complete sense. When a group of words simply follow one after another without making sense, that is simply a **word string**. When the group of words express a complete sense, that is called a **sentence**. (4) (13)

In the sentences below, the words describing the verbs are called adverbs.

My mom sings **beautifully.**
How does mom sing? **(beautifully).**
The baby sleeps **soundly.**
How does the baby sleep? **(soundly)**
I play with rubber ducky **quietly.**
How do I play with rubber ducky? **(quietly)**

Thus a **sentence** is a string of words that makes sense. A group of words without a complete thought is a **phrase.** We can have a noun phrase or a verb phrase. A **noun phrase** is a noun with its modifier(s). A **verb phrase** is a verb with its modifier(s).

THE SYNTAX RULE

The sequence of words in a sentence follows the **syntax rule.** The syntax provides the guideline for the words to arrange themselves in a sentence. It acts as a framework where the various parts of the sentence fit in.

WORDS

A sentence is made up of words. Let's now talk about words.

The simplest unit in a sentence is called a **word.** Words form the basic ingredients in a sentence. Words have inherent meanings by themselves, they could also combine with other words in a certain sequence to express different meanings. Words can also extend their meanings by adding small word parts at the beginning of the word called **prefix o**r at the end of the word called **suffix**. Two words can join together to form a new word called a **compound word**. A few examples clarify these terms.

Compound Words

Root	+	**Root**	=	**Compound Word**
sun	+	flower	=	sunflower
sun	+	rise	=	sunrise
sun	+	set	=	sunset
rain	+	coat	=	raincoat
rain	+	drop	=	raindrop
rain	+	fall	=	rainfall
snow	+	storm	=	snowstorm
snow	+	flake	=	snowflake
cow	+	boy	=	cowboy
pan	+	cake	=	pancake
fire	+	fly	=	firefly

butter	+	fly	=	butterfly
high	+	way	=	highway
white	+	house	=	White House
moon	+	light	=	moonlight
ginger	+	bread	=	gingerbread
lip	+	stick	=	lipstick

Words with suffixes

Regular verbs form past tense by affixing "d" or "ed" at the end of the word.

Little word parts affixed at the end of a word are called suffixes

Root	Suffix	New Word
jump	ed	jumped
plant	ed	planted
walk	ed	walked
play	ed	played
clap	ed	clapped
sail	ed	sailed
rent	ed	rented
melt	ed	melted

Words with suffixes

Little word parts affixed at the end of a word are called suffixes

Root	Suffix	New Word
teach	er	teacher
help	ful	helpful
kind	ness	kindness
child	hood	childhood
state	ment	statement
master	y	mastery
funny	est	funniest
tall	est	tallest
slow	ly	slowly
piano	ist	pianist
violin	ist	violinist
study	ious	studious
fast	er	faster

Words with prefixes
Little word parts affixed at the beginning of words are called prefixes.

Prefix	Root	New Word
re	new	renew
mis	understood	misunderstood
dis	interested	disinterested
de	compose	decompose
de	bug	debug
in	divisible	indivisible
in	door	indoor
bi	cycle	bicycle
tri	cycle	tricycle
tri	angle	triangle

Synonyms
Words with similar or identical meanings are synonyms.

beautiful	pretty	attractive	charming
plain	simple	unattractive	ugly
far	distant	long	remote
rich	wealthy	deep	abundant
difficult	hard	hazardous	dangerous
smart	bright	intelligent	brilliant
clean	clear	tidy	neat
funny	laughable	humorous	hilarious
help	aid	assist	support
happy	cheerful	gay	pleased
lost	diminished	removed	taken away
win	gain	plus	victory
extravagant	spendthrift	careless	wasteful
good	polite	considerate	honest
dirty	filthy	unclean	messy
friend	pal	companion	acquaintance
sad	blue	lonely	unhappy
flee	run away	escape	dash
girl	gal	maid	lass
boy	lad	guy	young man

Antonyms
Words with opposite meanings are antonyms.

night	day	rough	smooth
short	long	tall	short
sad	happy	heavy	light
fat	thin	large	small

strong	weak	pleasant	unpleasant
dark	light	sweet	sour
wet	dry	full	empty
rich	poor	sharp	dull
slow	fast	sink	float
awake	asleep	thick	thin
hot	cold	wild	tame
first	last	straight	crooked
few	plenty	fast	slow
full	empty	soft	hard
hot	cold	opaque	transparent
young	old	bottom	top
tight	loose	colorful	colorless

Homophones

Words that sound alike but are spelled differently and have different meanings are homophones.

sail (boat)	sale (merchandise)
die (end of life)	dye (color)
waist (body)	waste (garbage)
pain (hurt)	pane (window pane)
pause (stop)	paws (dog)
mane (horse's mane)	main (main event)
see (to look)	sea (ocean)
hi (greeting)	high (not low)
steel (building material)	steal (theft)
won (victor)	one (singular)
read (read a book)	reed (grass)
rice (food)	rise (get up)
blue (color)	blew (past tense of blow)

gem (jewel)	gym (exercise)
sent (past tense of send)	scent (perfume)
seem (looks like)	seam (stitch)
lie (don't tell a lie)	lye (caustic)

Homographs (Words that are spelled alike but have different meanings, may also sound differently in some cases).

fall (the season)	fall (fell, fallen)
bank (financial)	bank (river bank)
bow (bow tie)	bow (bow to the audience)
novel (book)	novel (new)
story (Three Bears)	story (floor)
tear (from the eye)	tear (needs mending)
bear (animal)	bear (shoulder the burden)
can (container)	can (ability, can do)a
whip (whip cream)	whip (punishment)
whistle (blow the whistle)	whistle (device for blowing sound)
turn (take turn)	turn (twirl around)
dress (wear a dress)	dress (dress a wound)
plant (green plant)	plant (work or manufacturing site)
base (each base in baseball)	base (base of triangle)
hand (fingers in the hand)	hand (to give)

LANGUAGE IS COMPLEX

We can see that language is complex. From the few elements called words, we can generate many more words by applying the rules of suffixes, prefixes and compound words. There are different forms for tenses of verbs. There are forms for singular or plural nouns. With a change in form there is a corresponding change in meaning. There are also words with the same form yet differ in meaning **(homographs)**.

The astonishing principle in language is that out of finite number of words an infinite number of thoughts can be generated. (4) (13) As the child matures to have absorbed the culture one learns that sentences can make a statement, a declarative sentence, ask a question, an interrogative sentence, express a command or request, an imperative sentence or express strong emotions, an exclamatory sentence. One can transform one form to another.

Types of sentences

The child is playing with his toys. (declarative)

What is the child doing? (interrogative)

Give the child something to play with. (imperative)

The child built a tower! (exclamatory)

The meaning in a sentence changes with the sequence of words.

Observing a four–year-old in a conversation, one sees that each response to a speaker is original, constructed on the spot, not previously heard spoken by someone else.

> Consider this example. A four year old exclaimed with joy upon seeing drawings of Santa Claus and Frosty, the Snowman in the newspaper. **"Look, the Christmas people!"**

> "Quite a bit of wildlife!" (a six year old's reaction upon seeing birds of different colors on his first visit to his backyard).

> "I'm full of joy," commented a five-year old as he showed pleasure after the Madrigal Dinner and now awaiting the choral concert to begin.

> Not knowing what an ice cream sandwich is called, he asked for a "brown, rectangular ice cream."

> At a labor-management negotiation with his mother, the six-year old stated where he stood, "I want green, rectangular dollars not round quarters."

> Thinking he knows all there is to know about the Nutcracker having danced "March of the Soldiers" at his school's production, he gave a critic's judgment, "They got it all wrong."

It is not a mere retrieval of pre-constructed sentences from his repertoire of sentences in storage. It is seen more as though the child has a storehouse of words with their corresponding meanings and rules that he can apply to produce an intelligent response. How does a child do this?

Noam Chomsky, (4) the foremost authority on linguistics, suggests that the child already has a built-in capacity to acquire new vocabulary, distill rules of grammar from what he has heard and apply these rules in conversation. This ability to acquire language quickly and flawlessly has been called by Chomsky **Universal Grammar. (4)** "Universal" is the term used because this capacity is inherent in all humans. Speech development comes just as naturally as cell division, a natural consequence of being a biological being. **Pinker (18)** characterizes speech development as like an instinct with the exception that with language some form of stimulus is necessary to trigger the onset of development.

Evolutionary biologists consider language as adaptation to communicate. Spoken language is the driving force in communication and a cohesive factor in cooperative endeavors. Construction projects of ancient times could not have been achieved without people talking to one another or to their teams. Language is indispensable in all human activities. (18)

The instinct to talk is inherent. A person talks even to himself, to the dog or to the plants. Humans are equipped with the instinct to listen, learn and understand language. This capacity for language was first described by **Darwin** in his book '**The Descent of Man.**' (7) It is inherent in the child to plow through and make sense of the noise in the world.

We need to applaud children for their spectacular achievement in acquiring speech quickly, flawlessly and perfectly. We also need to give them credit for re-inventing language in each generation to fit the needs of the time. Language bridges time and space. (4) (17) (18)

Reading and Writing

Writing and reading are the abstract forms of speaking and listening. What we experience, what we do can be described in words and can be communicated to another in speech. What can be spoken can be written. What is written can be read.

Our principle in teaching reading and writing is to follow the developmental sequence in speech acquisition. We believe that we learn to read the way we learned to talk just as we learn to walk before we can run.

We define writing as transcribing what we say into understandable signs. Reading is deciphering what the sign says. Writing is the abstract form of speaking just as reading is the abstract form of listening. Writing and reading go together as our means of written communication just as listening and speaking are our means of oral communication. Learning to read and write is simply learning to communicate in the abstract what we have been able to communicate orally. We replace signs that we hear with signs that we see.

Love of Learning Reading through Phonics Program Framework and Method

This book is about a program designed to teach reading and writing through phonics. The **first section** introduces the principles used in designing the **Program.** The **second section** is the **program** itself which may be used as a manual by the teacher, parent or mentor. Illustrations and manipulative card materials are available for purchase through the Love of Learning LLC.com. One may choose to draw outline figures and cut out letters as needed.

Program Framework

The framework of the **Program** may be summarized with the following statements:

1. We teach the key to reading, not words to read.
2. Anyone motivated to learn can learn to read at any age with appropriate instruction and materials. Just as one learns to speak

the language that one hears, one learns to read the language that one speaks.

3. Language learning is an interactive process. It begins at birth or even before birth. Talking, singing, reciting and reading to the learner promotes speech acquisition.

4. Learning to read does not begin with learning the names of the alphabet. Rather it begins with being familiar with the sound values that letters make.

5. Vocabulary building tied to comprehension is embedded in the process of learning sound values of letters of the alphabet. Along with phonemic awareness, phonics and fluency, we teach individuals to read in accordance with the guidelines published by the National Reading Panel.

6. There are 17 distinct lessons based on the phonics grouping identified by Rudolf Flesch in "Why Johnny Can't Read and What You Can Do About It." Depending on the individual and the amount of time spent with lessons, it is possible that one could read with this method in two years or less.

7. We borrowed ideas from the works of Maria Montessori (Montessori Method), Howard Gardner (Frames of Mind), Frank Laubach (Each One Teach One) and David Crystal (Spell It Out) in designing the program.

8. Success is seen as inspiring an individual to want to read, to love to read and fully participate in the life of our technologically advanced literate society.

A. The Key to Reading

The key to reading and writing is knowing how words are encoded and decoded. We do not assign 20 words to study overnight to read to the teacher the following day. This method encourages memorization associating word shape to what it says.

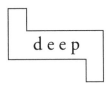

Memorization as a strategy has limitations. There are many words with basically the same shape.

Short-term memory has a limited number of available slots. When the memory capacity is exceeded, it kicks off a previously learned word in order to accommodate a new word being considered.

The complete list of letters drawn with their corresponding key words may be found on the alphabet chart.

The **Love of Learning Method** utilizes a different process which will be explained next.

First, the learner associates sound values for each letter symbol of the alphabet.

s *for snake*   m *for mountain*   r *for river*

Later in the **program**, one will be introduced to the sound values of letter clusters, two or more letters together representing a single sound.

ai *as in aim*   **ee** *as in eel*   **sh** *as in shell*   **oo** *as in moon*

The Process of Decoding

The first step in decoding is to look at the word and focus on the first letter on the left side of the word.

s u n.

The symbol **s** stands for the sound value of **"s"** as in **snake.**

The second symbol **u** stands for the sound of **"u"** as in **up.**

s u n.

The last symbol **n** stands for the sound of **"n"** as in **noodles.**

s u n.

By combining the symbols **s, u,** and **n** - sounding them in succession, we hear a familiar word - **"sun."**

We just illustrated the process of **decoding.**

The Process of Encoding

The process of **encoding** works in a similar manner.

Supposing we want to write the word **"sun."**

We pronounce the word **"sun"** and decide that the word begins with the sound value of **"s"** which we represent with the letter **"s."** We write the letter **"s."**

We help the student identify the next sound, the vowel **"u"** as it is not as easily discernible as the consonants. We write the letter **"u"** to the right of the first letter."

We continue sounding out the word and decide that it ends with the final sound value of **"n"** which we represent with the letter **"n."** We write the letter **"n"** to the right of **"u."** We have written the word **"sun."**

We make sentences using the word "**sun**."

> The **sun** is yellow.
> The **sun** is hot.

We encourage the learner to make his own sentence using the word **sun.**

The learner already knew the meaning of the word "sun." If a word proves to be new to the learner, we take the time to show what the word means with a picture, or an object or a simple description.

Segmenting and Blending

The process explained above consists of two parts:

1) breaking the word into its component parts and
2) blending the parts together to form the original word.

The process of breaking a word into its component sounds is called **segmenting.**

Blending the component sounds to say the word is called **blending**.

Segmenting and blending are the cornerstones of reading and writing. If we knew the sound values of all letter symbols and letter cluster symbols, we can decode any word. We can read everything.

The process may seem slow initially. However through practice and repetition, automaticity sets in and the learner decodes faster and faster until he decodes at the speed of **reading.**

Segmenting and blending are the prerequisite skills for reading and writing, not learning the names of the alphabet at this stage. Calling the letters by their names does not lead to hearing the sound of the entire word. In fact it merely adds another step unrelated to deciphering what the word says. Hearing isolated sounds of a word pronounced by a mentor followed by blending these sounds into a word by the learner is the first stepping stone in the reading process. **This is the missing step** too often neglected by mentors. We usually move from learning the alphabet to reading simple words

The first role of the mentor is to engage the learner in segmenting and blending activities. In the examples below, segment the word by saying it slowly or breaking the word into syllables or breaking the word into its component sounds. Remember, the learner is not reading at this point, only listening and speaking. Do not show the words you are segmenting.

Mentor Segments	Learner Blends
pop ... corn	popcorn
sun ... light	sunlight
um..brell...a	umbrella
Cin...de...re...la	Cinderella

pump...kin	**pumpkin**
rain...bow	**rainbow**
f...i...sh	**fish**
l...a...mp	**lamp**
c...an...dle	**candle**
gr...ee...n	**green**
dr...e...ss	**dress**
sl...ee...p	**sleep**

Once the learner can segment and blend orally, one is ready to learn to read and write.

Segmenting and blending continue to play significant roles in the reading process with this basic difference: component sounds previously spoken and listened to are now represented with letters of the alphabet. Blending sounds into words follows the same process.

Profiles of adult non-readers

Let's take a look at situations I personally observed of adults who could not read.

Adult Non-reader Case No. 1

Woman at church with hymnal

A woman consistently turned her hymnal upside down during church services. A fellow church member found out that the woman could not read. A friend referred her to a reading tutor who successfully taught her how to read. With that skill attained the woman stopped turning the hymnal upside down.

Adult Non-reader Case No. 2

Lady Toastmaster

As the Contest Master at a Toastmaster speech contest, I asked a lady to read the rules prior to the commencement of the contest. She stumbled on a few words. She struggled as she began to read the first rule. At that rate the contest could not start until sunset. I relieved her of this unpleasant task and asked someone else to take her place.

Adult Non-reader Case No. 3

Gentleman at the Workman's Compensation Clinic

A gentleman dressed in a suit approached me while I was waiting to be treated at the Workman's Compensation Clinic. He asked me to read a word on the form. I read it for him. He then told me what to write on the line. He then asked me to do the same for the next line and the next. I was convinced he could not read so I just filled in the whole form for him.

Adult Non-reader Case No. 4

<u>Osting's fingernail codes</u>

Osting played the correct music on cue at my father's campaign rallies. Everything worked well until my cousin discovered that Osting could not read. Osting marked the lids of boxes containing musical tapes with lines he scratched with his fingernails. To play a prank on Osting, my cousin tore off the lid with fingernail markings. Osting had no clue what to do. He did his best but ended up playing the wrong music at the wrong time. What a mess it was.

Back home, my mother taught Osting how to read using phonics. In no time he was reading the local weekly magazine in the vernacular.

Insufficient instruction as cause for reading deficiency

Learning to read is a complex issue. Not one cause can be solely attributed for a particular reading deficiency. However when one has not been taught to read, how do you expect one to read? Such is the case with Osting and the woman turning her hymnal upside down. In each case no reading instruction was given. Once it was provided, the problem was remedied.

In the case with the lady at the Toastmaster contest and the man at the Workman's Compensation Clinic, they had some instruction to read at the beginning level but received no further mentoring to be able to decode longer or unfamiliar words.

One needs to learn the complete set of phonics signs and learn them well to achieve fluency in letter recognition and sounding them out.

Now let's take a look at children who had initial difficulty in learning to read.

Cases of children with reading difficulty

Child Case No. 1

Did not know the sounds of the alphabet

Jimmy had been in Montessori preschool for four years. He had been coming to the language table for lessons regularly. His lesson consisted of tracing the sandpaper letter as in writing with his fingers, hearing the pure sound of the letter while looking at it. He was introduced to two letters at a time. After all these lessons, he calls any letter with whatever name he chooses. He could not associate any sound value to any letter he was presented. This continued until we devised keywords for easy recall for each letter. Handing him a picture of the keyword gave him an opportunity to pick up the keyword to match with the letter card.

The keyword chosen had an initial sound of the object and also resembled the shape of the letter.

m as in **mountain**

Simply hearing the sound value of the letter, looking and tracing the sandpaper letter were not sufficient to associate the sound with the shape. A picture of the object gave the abstract idea something concrete to hold on. It served as a handle with which to pull the object from storage.

Child Case No. 2

<u>Did not know how to break up words into sounds and blend them to say the original word</u>

Ken knew all the sound values of the letters of the alphabet. He could pick the correct letter card asked from the alphabet box. His problem was with segmenting and blending.

You say **m a n,** Ken says "monkey" or "elephant" or any word he could think at the moment. There was no relationship whatsoever with the segmented sounds and the blended word Ken said.

Ken had not made the connection between the segmented sounds to the word it says when blended.

To address this problem, we played the following:

1. I clapped four times, Ken said "four." I clapped seven times, Ken said "seven." No letter symbols nor numerals were used, just listening and speaking.
2. We played listen to the command then do the action.
   Wash your **h..a..nds."**
   Wash your **h..ai..r**
   st...a...nd"
   r...u...n to the door
   j...u...mp up and down
3. Touching a cup of coffee, say **"h...o...t."**
   Touching an ice cube say "**c...o...ld."**
4. I spread pictures of a **hat, map, can and nap**. I segmented each word and asked student to give the named picture.

c...a...n	(can)
h...a...t	(hat)
m...a...p	(map)
n...a...p	(nap)

Here the student had to choose the named picture among four to correspond to the segmented sounds. This process was missing in the student's repertoire of decoding skills. Once the student understood this concept, he was on his way to decoding and reading.

We continued segmenting and blending every day until school ended. Ken was still not reading at the end of the school year.

While on vacation a few weeks later, Ken's mother called long distance. She held the phone close to Ken so I could hear him read fluently. She said **he had been reading non-stop, they ran out of books.**

She remembered me telling her that reading will come in time because we had been doing lessons that will lead to reading. She said she heard it a few times. She wondered whether to believe me or not. Now, she does.

Child Case No. 3

<u>Committed to coloring progress record not to reading</u>

Lisa's new teacher asked her students to read to her one by one. Lisa was considered to be in fourth grade. She could not read one single word. The teacher looked at her records and saw that Lisa had successfully completed all self-checking tests up to fourth grade. The teacher asked Lisa to demonstrate how she worked with her workbook.

Lisa showed that she first "read" the story she was supposed to read in the workbook. She then took a blank form to write her answers to the multiple-choice questions. Once she had done this, she compared her answers to the master key available for student use on the shelf. She decided she passed the test and colored in the appropriate square on the record book. She would then do the next story in the series the next day. When all stories bearing the same color (belonging to the same series) had been read she promoted herself to the next color series. Throughout this process, Lisa had not read what the story was all about. She was more interested in coloring the squares in the record book and advancing to the next color in the program. Record keeping supplanted reading that it was supposed to promote.

We had to bring Lisa back to the fundamentals of the reading process:- segmenting, blending, reading and writing. We also had to listen to Lisa read every day.

HOW DO WE TEACH OTHERS TO READ AND WRITE?

If we need instruction to read and write, how should we teach others to read and write? We gained insights from a few selected educators and researchers:

Maria Montessori, Frank Laubach, Rudolf Flesch, David Crystal and Howard Gardner.

A brief bio of the five along with their unique contribution to the development of literacy or education in general follows.

Maria Montessori (11)

Dr. Maria Montessori, the first Italian woman physician, first observed that children institutionalized received no intellectual stimulation nor training in self-care. They were spoon-fed, dressed and left to simply lie around in bed all day. When the meal carts were wheeled in, she noticed that children showed excitement at the prospect of seeing food. This was interpreted in two different ways:

1) The orderlies compared the children to animals excited with food and nothing else.
2) Montessori saw the children as intelligent beings deprived of opportunity to develop and express their potential.

This observation prompted Montessori to develop materials and methods to teach children how to feed, dress and care for themselves and the environment. Further development of materials for the development and refinement of the senses took place in a "day care center" organized to get children constructively occupied to keep them from defacing the building while parents worked away from home.

Writing

The world was amazed to see self-disciplined, courteous and happy children as they moved from one activity to another in the "children's house." With the ease in learning names of geometric solids and geometric shapes, parents approached Montessori to move forward and teach their children how to read.

Montessori was aware how complex and difficult the reading process was and it was better for them to wait till their children go to school and learn to read from their teachers. The parents pressed Montessori to listen to their argument: everything seems easy with her method and learning to read is difficult for most children. Convinced with that argument, Montessori undertook research and development on teaching reading and writing appropriate for young children.

Strengthening the finger muscles to be engaged in writing was achieved through the various washing, polishing and cleaning activities in the Children's House.

Proper grasp of the pencil for writing was introduced and encouraged by picking up puzzle pieces by the knob to remove them from the board.

Children drew shapes by pushing the pencil against the outline of specially- designed metal shapes called metal insets. This helped with pencil control to make marks on paper. Filling in the shape with short parallel lines provided more writing practice than could have been accomplished with making vertical lines on lined paper.

Writing letters of the alphabet

Writing letters of the alphabet was divided into two parts: developing pencil control and learning to form the letters using the appropriate strokes.

Sandpaper letters on boards were traced with the first two fingers using the same strokes normally used by experienced writers. Writing with fingers gives one the practice of letter formation without the added burden of controlling the pencil.

Further practice in writing with the fingers was done on a sand tray.

Learning the shapes and sounds of the letters of the alphabet

One sandpaper letter pasted on a sturdy board was presented. The mentor traces the letter with the appropriate writing stroke. She pronounces the sound value of the letter. The presentation was repeated. A second letter was presented in the same manner.

A game is played between the mentor and the learner to reinforce letter-sound recognition. The brief lesson ends.

Letters previously taught would be reviewed the following day and new ones would be introduced. This routine was followed during each lesson.

Reading and writing

Multiple copies of letters are cut and organized in divided container. Letters are picked and sounded out one after another to spell a word.

    c   u   p   (cup)

A toy cup (or a picture of a cup) may be matched to the word. The same word may be written on the board.

Practice

With practice, the learner encodes and decodes words with ease. The learner writes spontaneously. The discovery that one can read leads to a surge of interest in reading non-stop.

Practices adopted:

The following practices have been adopted by the program:
Use of sandpaper letters for tactile experience
Incorporating movement into the lesson
Combined use of visual, auditory and kinesthetic experiences in lessons
Simplicity of total reading scheme – one lesson at a time, review, reinforcement

Breaking down complex task into several simpler steps: writing with fingers to writing with pencil
One-to-one teaching-learning session with student
Joy of learning

FRANK LAUBACH (10)

Discovery of the Laubach reading method

Frank Laubach, a trained minister, volunteered to serve with his bride as a missionary in the Philippines. They were assigned to work with the Moslems called Moros in the southern island of Danao. He read books on Philippine history and culture on his way to his destination. He worked hand in hand with a fellow missionary, a native from a neighboring province. They realized that they needed to learn to speak the language of the people to begin their work.

There was no dictionary nor anything in print in the vernacular. Enlisting the help of friends they have made in the island, they wrote local words with the Latin alphabet. His fellow missionary companion learned to speak the local language quickly because his native tongue was somewhat similar to the local language. Dr. Laubach learned to speak the vernacular soon after.

They found out that the natives wanted to read the bible but they did not know how to read. This necessitated a closer study of the language. They discovered that the language is simpler than English, it only had 12 consonants and 7 vowels. With the Latin alphabet, they had enough letters to represent all the sounds of the language with a few letters to spare.

Laubach invented a method of teaching to read. He made large charts showing keywords for the letters. Pairing the consonant with each vowel, one produces syllables. One can then see words that can be formed from the syllables. It was a thrill for the Moros that they can read what they speak. People wanted to learn to read. It only took a day or two to master the reading system. The news spread far and wide, people travelled to be taught how to read. Dr. Laubach opened a training institute for teachers to accommodate more students. Teachers were paid by the mission for each successful student.

They wrote the first issue of their newspaper. Someone gave them a printing press so they could print their newspaper. The chiefs (*dato and sultan*) could read but the general public could not. The chiefs could see the newspaper serve as a vehicle for all kinds of information – about health, agriculture and even the price of vegetables. This awakened an interest in learning to read.

BENEFITS OF LITERACY

Literacy was seen as a benefit personally, politically and sociologically.

When one can read what is written in the agreement, one can no longer be cheated into paying more than what the contract says tying one for life in indebtedness. Literacy was seen as a way out of poverty.

Politically, everyone who can read and write can vote. Officials elected could determine how the people may be governed. With elections, the balance of power could shift from the few, the elite, to the masses with an increased population of literate citizens.

Sociologically, dissemination of information is faster and more efficient with the publication of newspapers than can be accomplished with face to face communication once contact has been made with other people. How to take care of one's health, how to have higher yield in the rice field, how to control tuberculosis – these are some of the benefits for knowing how to read and write.

Each One Teach One

The enthusiasm for literacy continued. It was funded by the mission.

When there was a downturn in economic conditions, the mission could no longer support the literacy campaign. The teachers had to be terminated from their employment. One Chief came up with a suggestion. Let everyone who could read and write teach another and keep the movement going. The idea was well received. From then on, the literacy campaign adopted the slogan, "Each one teach one."

Mentoring new students was beneficial to the mentor as well. With each successful mentoring, the mentor gains a deeper insight on the material and method. Through teaching one shares one's skill and participates in the mission of creating world literacy.

World Literacy

Dr. Laubach continued his work of spreading literacy across the globe. He used the same method in every place:

Work cooperatively with local educators and interested citizens.

Figure out the spoken language vocabulary and structure.

Figure out the best possible keyword for each letter.

Make large charts showing keyword, picture and syllables.

Each one teach one.

Use gentle voice tone in teaching, no harsh words nor put-downs.

Dr. Laubach travelled to different countries applying his method, creating new charts particularly designed to teach reading the language of the country. He won the admiration and support of famous leaders – Mahatma Gandhi, Rabindranath Tagore and Jawaharlal Nehru. Wherever he was, he was teaching, transforming men and women into literate citizens and inspiring leaders to continue the literacy campaign.

Rudolph Flesch

Rudolf Flesch wrote a book in 1955, "Why Johnny Can't Read and What You Can Do About It." The book looked critically at how we teach children to read in our schools. He supported his views with classroom observations and interviews with authors and authorities on the field of teacher education and teaching reading. The main points of Flesch's argument are summarized in the book.

Why Johnny Can't Read

Beginning in 1930, educators abandoned teaching reading through phonics. Instead of teaching the alphabetic code as the avenue for deciphering what a word says, one was taught to guess and memorize what words mean. This method was meant to save children from the drudgery of learning the sounds of letters and letter clusters.

This method was also dubbed as the **look – and – say method.** It was also the **word reading method.** No one was taught the sound of letters. One was encouraged to guess what the word might say by looking at context clues or pictures on the page.

The reason Johnny couldn't read was because no one had shown him how.

The learner taught with phonics learned to read not guess.

Once he knew how to read he could read everything.

Effects of using word reading method as reading instruction

Emphasis shifted to the visual rather than the auditory means of deciphering information. Students needed to look at the whole word, its shape, its length – not on the specific letters within the word. The teacher identifies the word for the student.

Words had to be repeated several times on the printed reader to reinforce reading selected words.

Vocabulary had to be reduced to keep the number of words within prescribed limits.

Undue word repetition made the "story" sound unnatural and boring.

Student was limited to reading carefully crafted readers. This deprived them of being able to read and enjoy children's literature such as folk tales, fairy tales, mythology, etc.

Professional advocates of the word method were strongly convinced of its efficiency. No argument could make them switch their position. Textbooks on how reading should be taught discussed only the word reading method.

Students were exposed to word reading from first grade through high school

Meanwhile parents complained to their principal that their children could not read. They were given the pat answer that with time everything will be alright.

How do we teach Johnny to read?

We teach Johnny how to write and read at the same time.

We teach spelling and reading as two sides to the same coin. When we can spell, we can read what we just spelled.

We teach phonics systematically, not as a sporadic activity engaged every now and then. We begin with teaching to recognize and write each symbol, the letters of the alphabet. We do not teach the names but rather we teach the sounds of the letters.

We also teach the sound of letter clusters, a group of two or more letters of the alphabet with a unique sound. Once we can recognize the whole list of symbols, we have the rudiments for reading and writing. We just need to practice to make the task automatic.

The economy of learning to read through phonics

There are only 26 letters of the alphabet. With these, we can combine several letters to make additional symbols to completely code our language. There are 44 total phonemes, units of sounds. There may be duplicate forms to represent some phonemes. With these limited number of units of sounds and symbols, we can write and read any word in the English language. Compare that to the seemingly endless task of learning to read so many words per year.

The advantages of learning to read with phonics

Students who learned to read with phonics read fluently and with understanding. Students who learned to read with word reading, struggle to read word for word as they try to recall what that particular word says.

Generally students taught to read with phonics are ahead by a year in academic achievement compared to the average student.

Students taught with phonics will try to decipher a new word they encounter while those taught through whole word method simply stop with no strategy for figuring out what the word says.

Last word of advice

Parents can teach their children to read with phonics.

The first thing to do is to clear the mind of the bad habit of reading through guessing which is not reading at all.

Follow the lesson outlined by Rudolf Flesch and see that your child can read at the end of summer.

Author's Note: The Love of Learning LLC have drawn materials to illustrate each phoneme (sound-symbol) in color available through Love of Learning LLC.com.

David Crystal

David Crystal, a British linguist, an author of over 100 books, a recognized authority on linguistics, gave an overview of the various spelling changes of English words over centuries to address events that impacted on the English language.

The Anglo-Saxons living in the British Isles had a writing system using their Rune alphabet to transcribe their spoken language. Roman influence began when the Romans occupied the land around **400 B.C.** Through trade and mingling of cultures, several Latin words were assimilated into the English vocabulary.

Spell It Out

In his book, "**Spell it Out,**" David Crystal tried to answer the question **why do we spell this word this way?** He chronicled various events impacting on the English language and how the Anglo-Saxons continuously struggled to spell these new loan words using the new English alphabet.

Problem caused by adopting the Roman alphabet

The Anglo-Saxons adopted the Roman alphabet to replace the Rune alphabet in use.

The first problem seen was that there were only 23 letters of the Roman alphabet and there were about 44 sounds of the English language. This meant that several words could not be spelled with the Latin alphabet. The monks and the scribes went to work on addressing this problem.

Combining two letters to make a new sound was one strategy.

Compounding the problem was the influence of the French who conquered and occupied the land with the **Norman Invasion in 1096.**

Consonants

In the Anglo-Saxon alphabet some letters may have more than one sound.

The letter "g" may have the hard sound as in "go" or the soft sound as in "gem." To clarify when one sound or the other is applied, a rule was verbalized:

The letter "g" when followed by "a," "o," or "u," it may have the sound of "g" as in "go"

The letter "g" when followed by "e," "i," or "y," may have the sound of "g" as in "gem."

Long Vowels

How do you represent long vowel sounds? Several strategies were tried.

Doubling the letters would make it longer: oo (moon) ee (keep).

Silent "e" at the end of a word was a long vowel marker. The vowel that precedes silent "e" has a long vowel sound.

Not ---- note

In a pair of vowels representing a long vowel, (deer) one vowel may be replaced with another vowel. (dear)

meet ---- meat

reed ---- read

see ---- sea

Homophones

The above examples show where two words sound alike but have different meanings. These words are called **homophones.** (sail and sale)

<u>**Homographs**</u> – words with the same spelling but differ in meaning and sometimes in pronunciation.

staff (people employed) and staff (support stick)

play (children's game) and play (theater)

dress (dress a wound) and dress (garment)

Double Consonant Rule

A vowel followed by a double consonant is a short vowel.

A vowel followed by a single consonant is a long vowel.

<u>Short vowel</u>	<u>Long vowel</u>
tunnel	tuna
hopping,	hoping
holly	holy

Note that instead of doubling "k" use "ck".
Words ending in p, b, t, d, g, m, and n follow the double consonant rule.
Double consonant rule applies to words ending in f, s, z, l and r.

French spelling impact on English

From the 11th century on, several reforms were initiated by the French.

New letters replaced old ones: gh, (in some cases it was silent as in night, in others it was pronounced as **f** as in laugh).

Preference for ce instead of s, dance, fence.

French spelling prevailed over Old English (rich/ritch).

French appeal prevailed – boutique

HOWARD GARDNER

Frames of Mind by Howard Gardner

Reading and mathematics have been used as the primary measuring sticks for school achievement. John Gardner in his book, "Frames of Mind" showed the reader that there are other dimensions of addressing life's situations in one's own creative fashion. He calls these avenues for creative expression as the human intelligences. The intelligences mentioned by Howard Gardner are:

Language – sensitivity to words and word usage to convey desired message linguistically

Musical – sensitivity to melody, rhythm, sound quality and how one may use these elements in a musical composition

Logical-Mathematical – possessing an ardent desire to understand and explain nature

Spatial – capacity to perceive objects in space and imagine its transformation due to rotation or translation

Bodily-Kinesthetic-portrays a well-developed sense of balance and fine motor control

Personal – intrapersonal_–able to get in touch with one's feeling and wisely choose whether to get more involved or withdraw from a given situation.

Personal – interpersonal – the ability to detect the mood, temperament, intentions of people around one's self and to act accordingly

Sensing how one sees the world gives others an insight on how to relate to that person.

Language as the primary intelligence

Howard Gardner sees language as the primary intelligence endowed to human beings. Whereas not all can play music or perform gymnastic feats or paint works of art, everyone can speak. Nature has endowed human beings with flexibility in its development. Should some organ or region of the system be impaired or obstructed, its function will be taken over by another organ or another region in the system to allow acquisition of speech to proceed as normal as possible. This amazing property is possible due to the process of canalization –a process of ushering flow of information along a path of least resistance established over a period of time. The analogy of conveying water along a predetermined structure effortlessly is graphically clear.

Several components of language may be identified:

Phonology – the sound of words

Semantics – the meaning of words

Syntax – the word order in a sentence or phrase

The writer or speaker chooses the words to convey one's message.

The purpose of the speech or **pragmatics** could be one of the following:

To persuade to take a certain course of action

To describe

To explain

<u>Final points to remember:</u>

Let us remember how we communicate orally. We intake information through listening and convey our response through speaking.

Let us not forget that writing stems from speaking.

APPLYING INTELLIGENCES IN TEACHING READING AND WRITING

The book **"The Multiple Intelligences of Reading and Writing" by Thomas Armstrong** leads us to ask two questions:

1. In general how do these intelligences help us reach students struggling with literacy learning?
2. Specifically how does one use each intelligence to connect with a learner with a strength in any one of these intelligences to achieve literacy learning?

Generally, a student experiencing difficulty in remembering phoneme-symbol association and retention, may experience relief and even enjoyment if the teacher or mentor uses music, art, creative movement, or the natural world in introducing sound-symbol associations. Lessons become more interesting when emotional expression is included in the reading of stories or a story is being dramatized with the class.

> To the student, the specific intelligence is one's home base. One feels at home with this area in the same way that fish swims perfectly acclimated in water. It feels like wearing clothes that comfortably fit the wearer, not too tight, not too loose, it's just right.

> One has basic familiarity with the language being used to teach. Trying to understand the teacher speaking a different language

while trying to learn a new concept is doubly more difficult than being taught in the language that one speaks.

One has a natural aptitude for learning in the field of one's strength. Learning comes easily when we sing a song or clap the rhythm of new words or concepts which demonstrates our affinity for music and movement.

With the various intelligences in mind, why don't we include these intelligences in our repertoire of teaching skills? Perhaps, we have not had enough modeling from other educators to accept these modes of teaching as acceptable models. Perhaps we have not thought more deeply about these intelligences to be convinced that not only do these teaching modes lend variety to our routine, these also become necessary to reach some students.

Let me briefly identify these intelligences and associate them with some activities:

Linguistic - use to inform, to explain, persuade to take a stand

Logical-mathematical - the learner as scientist, problem-solver

Spatial-visual - the learner as image maker

Bodily-kinesthetic - link between physical movement and language

Musical - use elements of music to distinguish one phoneme from another

Interpersonal- writing as a social action

Intrapersonal - writing as a means to get in touch with our feelings

Naturalist - learning from nature

Here is an example of enriching the curriculum through using the intelligences described.

Author's note: The author offers the following interpretation on the role of the various intelligences in teaching literacy in the classroom through an integrated lesson.

Play the recording of Tchaikovsky's "Waltz of the Flower." (***music***). Hand students a couple of scarves and let them sway to the music with the scarves. They may move around the room.

(bodily-kinesthetic)

Teach the initial blend **fl** using a card bearing the **fl** symbol and introduce it as having the **fl** sound as in **flower.**

Arrange a few pots with flowers in them in the center of a table. Have children sit around the table on chairs. Allow students to note that some flowers are tall, some are short in height.

This compares to the height of letters. Some are tall **like b, d, f, h, k, l** and **t.**

Other letters are short like **a, c, e, i, m, n, o, r, s, u, v, w, x,** and **z.**

Some letters are short and go below the line like **g, j, p, q** and **y.** *(visual)*

> **Letters considered tall are: b, d, f, h, k, l, t**
>
> **Letters of low height: a, c, e, i, m, n, o, r, s, u, v, w, x, z**
>
> **Short letters with tails that go below the line: g, j, p, q, y**

Encourage students to create verses about flowers.

> They may talk about how beautiful flowers are.

They come in red (r), pink (p), (nk), yellow and blue (ue).

Thank you, flowers. *(writing a poem, linguistic).*

Use colored cards to show the consonants, **(p, r, y)** consonant blend (**bl**) and consonant digraph (**nk**). *(linguistic)*

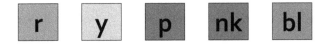

Discuss that flowers become fruits. Draw a chart to show the stages or development from seed to plant to flower to fruit. *(**Science, logico-mathematical**)*

Discuss how flowers make you feel. (***Intrapersonal***).

Talk to the flower as one would talk to a dear friend. (***Interpersonal***).

Have a round table discussion on why flowers are pretty? What is the function of flowers to the plant? (*Flowers are the reproductive organs of plants. The bright colors or special scent of flowers invite insects to come and drink its nectar. After a quick visit with one flower, the insect goes from one flower to another and repeats the process several times. With each visit, the insect gathers pollen from one flower and drops them to another as it moves from flower to flower. This effects pollination which when fertilized marks the beginning of a new cycle of new life for the plant. (naturalist)*

From the examples above, expanding the curriculum to include music, science, art, movement, nature as we try to teach letter-sound recognition is enjoyable and enriching for both the teacher and the student. The practice accomplishes two things:

It offers a wide range of activities that may capture the interest of the student.

One is led to the study of art, music, science, dance in an inter-related manner, each field reinforcing another.

The study of linguistic skills is reinforced seven-fold through engaging in art, music, dance and science. Each reinforcement strengthens previous learning. The net effect is adding a new dimension of learning with each reinforcement. Each dimension helps the learner acquire linguistic skills with less effort than would have been possible with concentrating only on linguistic products.

Let us not forget that before we had writing, we only used oral language and hand gestures to communicate.

Before there was writing using the alphabet, we used picture drawings which later evolved to Egyptian hieroglyphics.

Music in the form of rhythms with instruments and along with dance or movement served to unify the community through rituals.

Before we knew what we call today as science, we looked at the sun, moon and stars to plan when to plant our crops.

Language using the letters of the alphabet came as a recent human invention when compared to the practice of art, music, dance and learning from nature. It is therefore logical that using these other intelligences is like walking on a well-trod road, familiar to us which can serve as bridges to literacy.

Another set of guidelines

Aside from the insights we derived from the works of scholars and researchers discussed in the previous section, I want to introduce the basic themes espoused by the federal government to address the nation's reading deficiency.

A NATION AT RISK

United States. National Commission on Excellence in Education. (1983). A nation at risk: the imperative for educational reform: a report to the Nation and the Secretary of Education, United States Department of Education. Washington, D.C.: The Commission: [Supt. of Docs., U.S. G.P.O. distributor],

On April 1983, a landmark document was published by the blue-ribbon members of the National Commission on Excellence in Education. This report was written after an 18-month study by a special commission assembled to study the nature of the deficiencies in our school system and what we can do to address it. It was dubbed as the imperative for school reform.

The impetus for producing quality and competitive products have waned from the days immediately after the launching of Sputnik. This trend parallels a steady decline of scores in various standardized tests. A good number could not read proficiently and lacked higher order skills expected among high school graduates. Business leaders and military administrators had to provide extensive training in literacy, mathematics and science among new recruits which proved to be expensive. These new employees were not ready to assume responsible positions due to these deficiencies.

If this trend continues, the nation will be at risk. At a time when greater technical and technological skills are needed for the jobs of a highly technological society, we find a population unable to meet society's demand.

America could lose its position as the leader of the free world. Other industrialized countries have placed education as its primary goal. Students in those countries spend more hours a day and more days a year in scholarly pursuits. We have relaxed the rigor of the curriculum. Students have been allowed to substitute elective courses for required courses.

Teachers have not been viewed with high regard. As a result of this perception, a good number of teachers have been drawn from students with mediocre academic standing. More effort needs to be made to attract more academically prepared students to go into teaching. The public needs to act together to seize the vision that gave the spirit that inspires excellence. With renewed cooperation and hard work together, we can build up the nation's strength with faith in today's trust and hope in tomorrow's outcome.

The Reading Excellence Act

19 a) The Reading Excellence Act was a competitive grant program awarding grants to States for proposing a good research-based method for improving the teaching of young children from K-3 to read.

It proposed that programs carry out the following purposes:

Teach every child to read by the end of third grade.

Provide children in early childhood with the readiness skills and support they need to learn to read once they enter school.

Expand the number of high-quality family literacy programs.

Provide early intervention to children who are at risk of being identified for special education inappropriately.

Base instruction, including tutoring, on scientifically based reading research.

The Reading Excellent Act, includes a definition of reading that must be used by all participants applying for a grant. The definition is reproduced below.

Reading is a complex system of deriving meaning from print that requires:

Skills and knowledge to understand how phonemes, or speech sounds, are connected to print.

Ability to decode unfamiliar words

Ability to read fluently

Sufficient background knowledge and vocabulary to foster reading comprehension

Development of appropriate active strategies to construct meaning from print

The development and maintenance of a motivation to read

NATIONAL READING PANEL

(19 b) National Reading Panel was established to: a) review research on how children learn to read, b) determine most effective method for teaching to read, c)describe ways in getting this information to schools.

Furthermore, The Reading Panel strongly suggests that regardless of method used in teaching to read, a proficient reader seeks to develop the following skills: phonemic awareness, phonics, fluency, guided oral reading, teaching vocabulary and reading comprehension. A brief description of these skills follow.

Phonemic awareness – the knowledge that spoken words can be broken into smaller sounds called phonemes. The word caterpillar has four distinct sounds.

Phonics – Letters of the alphabet have sounds. When blended together, certain sounds say a word. Other sounds are represented by a cluster of two or more letters to say a distinct sound.

Fluency – decoding letter-sounds in a word and blending them together to say a word becomes more fluent with practice until automaticity sets in.

Guided oral reading – reading to a mentor and getting feedback helps in gaining reading proficiency.

Teaching vocabulary words – teaching new words as they occur in a story or spending time in teaching new vocabulary before reading a story are ways in fostering knowledge of new words.

Reading comprehension strategies – include ways to improve or enhance understanding what we read. Retelling orally or summarizing what we read are ways of showing understanding of what we just read.

TREE OF READING

Let's visualize the reading program as a tree. The tree begins with the roots as the foundation. The roots give rise to the trunk which in turn gives rise to the branches where the leaves are attached.

The roots stand for phonemic awareness, activities to heighten the speaking-listening - thinking awareness without trying to teach letter sound and symbol. This includes singing, reciting poems, listening to stories, making up stories, rhyming, Lesson 1, clapping the number of syllables in a word, Lesson 2, segmenting and blending the sounds in a word, Lesson 3.

The trunk stands for the alphabet, the building blocks of words. Sounds of letters, phonemes, are taught, not the names of letters. The lower case, not the upper case is taught at this point. Movement is integrated with visual and auditory activities.

The branches represent the families of words we can produce and read by combining the letters of the alphabet.

We will teach these lessons one lesson at a time, allowing mastery through review and application.

A diligent student progressing at the rate of one lesson a week will complete the program in 72 weeks. If one tries to learn two lessons a week, mastery will take place in one year. An adult or older student spending summer with daily lessons will be able to read at the end of summer.

It is not how fast can one complete the program, rather how interested one has become in reading with every new code learned.

It is not important how fast can one complete the program rather how interested in reading one has become.

TREE OF READING

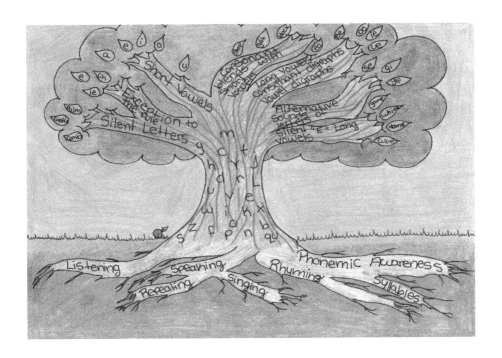

ROOTS

The **roots** stand for phonemic awareness, activities to heighten the speaking-listening-thinking awareness without the use of letter sound-symbol recognition. This includes singing, reciting poems, listening to stories, making up stories. Other lessons include rhyming, clapping the number of syllables in a word, and segmenting and blending the sounds in a word.

Root: Phonemic Awareness

The tree begins with the **root,** the foundation. The root symbolizes phonemic awareness. At this stage, no letter symbols are introduced, that comes later with the phonics stage. One can mentally delete, add or replace a sound with another phoneme.

Here we recite poems, listen to stories, sing songs, engage in water play, sand play engage in matching games and art activities. We visit museums, libraries, the zoo. We play in the park and at the beach. All these activities give us opportunities to expand our vocabulary, develop our visual, manual and auditory skills - all are prerequisites to writing and reading.

In phonemic awareness, we build on the verbal competence already mastered by the learner to move on towards learning the next steps.

Three phonemic awareness lessons included in the program are:

1. rhyming
2. counting the number of syllables
3. segmenting and blending

Lesson 1: Rhyming

We engage the learner with rhyming (Lesson 1) to recognize word elements that sound alike. Words with the same ending sound or whose final syllables sound alike are said to rhyme. While engaging in rhyming poems or songs, we build vocabulary, we become sensitized to similarities and differences of sounds and practice fluency in articulation.

1. **Rhyming words have similar or identical sounds of word endings.**

We can find words that rhyme with colors.

I have a friend and her name is Sue

Her favorite color is the color blue.   {**Sue rhymes with blue.**}

Here comes the queen

All dressed in green.   {**Queen rhymes with green.**}

With phonemic awareness one can recognize the phoneme that is not like the others.

Example: cat bat mat sun {<u>sun</u> does not sound like the rest of the words.}

With phonemic awareness one can recognize the phonemes (units of sound) that are identical to a given phoneme. Example: mop {hop, stop, drop, cop}

Lesson 2: Counting the Number of Syllables in a Word

Words may have one, two or more syllables. We introduce the concept of syllables so that learners can conceptualize where one word ends and the next one begins.

Syllables are marked by the natural break in the pronunciation of a word. By listening to how a word is pronounced, we can count the number of syllables in a word. <u>Lesson 2</u> gives us the vehicle to practice counting the number of syllables in a word. The teacher says the word and the student says the number of syllables it has.

Counting (clapping) the number of syllables one hears in a word.

Carrot has two syllables.
Elephant has three syllables.

We can count the number of syllables ---

> in one's name,
> days of the week
> significant words in a story
> names of countries, continents, lakes, geographical landmarks

Lesson 3: Segmenting and Blending

<u>Reading is decoding</u>. It is breaking down a word "cat" into its component sounds <u>(analysis)</u> "c" "a" "t" then blending the sounds together to sound like a familiar word "cat" <u>(synthesis)</u>. These two steps form the backbone of the phonics method of learning to read. To prepare for this phase, we introduce in phonemic awareness the step of segmenting a word we say verbally without the added difficulty of looking at letters or remembering what a letter sounds. Here, the teacher says the separate sounds of a word and the learner blends them together in one's head and says the word. One hands the object named or performs the action required.

Sample words to segment are printed on cards for the mentor.

Segmenting is breaking a word into its component parts (phonemes).

4. Blending is putting the separate sounds together to form the word.

Example:

b.oa.t	boat
ba.na.na	banana

5. Deleting or removing a given phoneme from a word

Example:

What is a **cowbo**y without a cow? **boy**

What is a **raincoat** without the rain? **coat**

6. Adding a phoneme to a word changes a word.

Example:

What's a **flower** in the **sun**? **sunflower**

What's a **bow** in the **rain**? **rainbow**

7. Replacing a phoneme with another

Example:

Start with **pancake.** Replace **pan** with **cup.** You get **cupcake.**

Start with **football.** Replace **foot** with **basket.** You get **basketball.**

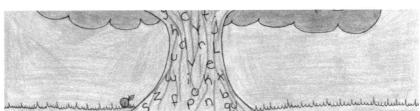

Trunk

The **trunk** stands for the alphabet, the building blocks of words. Sounds of letters, phonemes, are taught, not the names of letters. The lower case, not the upper case is taught at this point. Movement is integrated with visual and auditory activities.

Let's go to the original alphabet chart. There are 26 letters, three are not counted (3). We have duplicate "k" sound in "c" so we count "k" and leave "c" as an alternate sound for the "k" sound. The letter "q" is considered a blend of "k" and "w." "q" is paired with "u" to form the sound of "kw."

The letter "x" is a blend of "k" and "s." We do not count "x" in our tally of sounds. Not counting "c," "q," and "x" leaves us with **23** sounds in the alphabet.

Adding up the number of distinct sound units (phonemes):

Number of Phonemes in English
(perceptually distinct sound units)

Category	Number
single letters	23
long vowels + $\overline{oo}$ + $\breve{oo}$	7
consonant digraph	7
diphthong	3
r-controlled vowel	4
Total	**44**

HOW TO TEACH LETTER
SOUND-SHAPE RECOGNITION

While we focused solely on speech sound to represent words with phonemic awareness, we now have the use of letter symbols to spell words. Letter-symbols used to write names, places, dates, agreements on documents lend permanence to the record whereas speech disappears as soon as it has been spoken.

The author has created a unique set of materials designed to teach letter-sound correspondences. The **Love of Learning LLC** materials will now be described and demonstrated on its use in teaching recognition, retention and spelling.

Materials

Based on Dr. Montessori's work that we learn through the senses and through movement, we have the following materials:

A set of lower case sandpaper letters, each one pasted on Masonite boards, vowels on blue, consonants on red

Alphabet chart showing letters and their corresponding keywords

Each keyword object has the initial sound of the target letter. It also resembles the shape of the letter. We have "c" as in "cat" with the image of a cat seated to resemble the letter "c." The letter "s" is illustrated

75

with the keyword "snake" and is shown with the letter "s" shaped like a "snake."

Presentation:

With two fingers of the dominant hand, trace the sandpaper letter "c" the way one would normally write the letter. This teaches the proper stroke in writing the letter without the added burden of controlling the pencil. Find the colored picture card for the letter "c" and the keyword picture "cat." Say, "This says "c" for cat. Line three cards in a row from left to right: keyword picture, sandpaper letter, colored letter card.

Repeat the process to introduce the second letter, "s."

Play the game of "Where is "c" for "cat"?"

"Where is "s" for "snake?"

Remove keyword pictures and ask learner to match them with the sandpaper letters.

Remove sandpaper letters and ask learner to match them with the keyword pictures.

Ask for each card one at a time:

"Give me the picture of "cat." Give me the picture of "snake."

Give me the letter "c." Give me the letter "s."

When learner has shown accuracy to point letter asked, ask learner to identify letter, "What is this?" Here we are asking learner to pronounce the sound of the letter, an oral response. Previously, we only asked for a motor response.

Record date and letters taught in learner's notebook

In succeeding days, review letters taught and teach two new letters.

Engage learner in art activities to reinforce letter recognition: finger painting, making letters with play dough, writing with soap suds, writing on sand tray, etc.

Review all letters that have been taught before teaching new ones.

Encourage writing on chalk board with chalk, write with a wet sponge on chalk board, write with colored marker, crayon. Engage in rainbow writing, writing over written letters with different colors of the rainbow.

Building fluency with letter recognition

There are several ways to develop fluency in symbol-sound association:

1. games of finding letters from the alphabet chart
2. naming the letters along with their keywords in sequence as they appear on the chart
3. weave a story for each group of letters

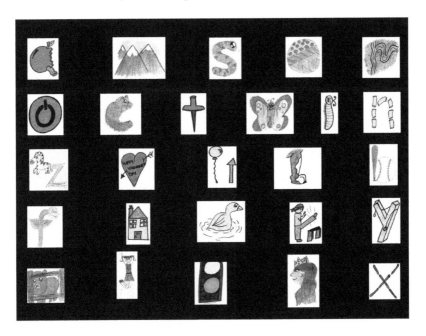

Building fluency with letter recognition

There are several ways to practice sounding out the letters to develop fluency and accuracy. One method is to weave a story for each group of letters. Here are some examples. You can make your own story.

z   u   **m**   a   e

I walked on a **zig-zag** road **up** the **mountain** to eat an **apple**, an **egg**, some

n   **v**

noodles on **Valentine's** Day.

s   o   **r**   **i**   **w**

A **snake** was lying **on** the grass beside the **river** watching **insect wings** fly

f

among the **flowers.**

j   **k**   **b**   **y**   **x**

I **jump** to **kick** the **ball** and **play** with a **yoyo** and **six sticks.**

h   **l**   **c**   **p**   **d**

I live in my **house** by the **lake** with my pet **cat, pig** and **duck.**

g i   **q u**

Go in and meet the **queen** today.

The **branches** represent families of words we can form combining the letters of the alphabet (list of lessons adopted from Flesch's "Why Johnny Can't Read and What You Can Do About It).

Branches

Word families in the Love of Learning LLC **Program.**

Words with short vowels

Short vowel words with blends

Words with long vowels

Consonant digraphs

Diphthongs

Words with r-controlled vowels

Words with silent "e" as a long vowel marker

Other sounds of "g," "c," and "s"

Multi-syllable words ending in le

Multi-syllable words ending in y

Double consonant rule

Silent letters

Exceptions to the rule

HOW TO TEACH READING SINGLE WORDS

	consonant	vowel	consonant
	C	V	C

c a t →	c	a	t
m o p →	m	o	p
c u p →	c	u	p

Purpose:

The purpose in this lesson is to analyze the initial consonant sound, the middle vowel and the final consonant sound for each word, to represent each sound with a letter card, blend the sounds to say the word represented by the picture card.

Pre-requisites:

1. Extensive experience with oral segmenting and blending (Lesson 3)
2. Fluency in recall of letter-sound association
3. Established left to right orientation

Practical Considerations:

1. A composition notebook for each child for recording lessons received
2. A divided tray for holding word building materials
3. Crayon
4. Pencil
5. Open shelf to provide easy access to materials

Materials:

<u>The materials include 3 sets of each of the following:</u>
a) Words with short a (ă), short e (ĕ), short i (ĭ), short o (ŏ), short u (ŭ), and final (ck).
b) Each set includes a basic teaching-working unit, two (2) check-up cards and a card of additional words to read
c) The teaching unit includes four picture cards, four word cards, individual letter cards to spell the four words.

Procedure:

The same procedure is followed for working with each set and is outlined below. (Illustrated with set 5a).

1. Line up picture cards horizontally.

Identify each picture for vocabulary check-up.
Teacher says: c-a-t. Student blends sounds and says "cat," picks picture of "cat" and hands it to the teacher.

Continue segmenting and blending pictures until all cards have been picked.

2. Line up cards vertically into columns of word cards, vowels and consonants.

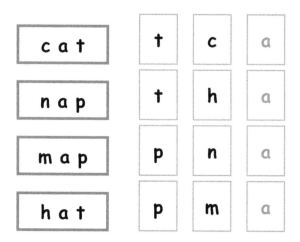

3. Select one of the picture cards, place it on the rug. Sound out initial sound of the word. Pick the corresponding letter card and place it to the right of the picture card.

Sound out the next sound which is a vowel. Pick the vowel and place it to the right of the first letter.

Sound out the final sound and pick its corresponding letter. Place it to the right of the vowel.

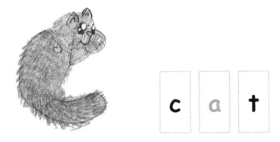

Blend the letters from left to right and pronounce the word. Find the matching word card from the column of word cards and place it under the spelled word.

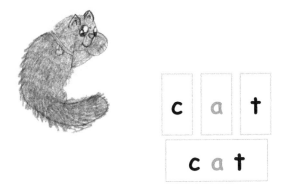

Rule: Short Vowel in a Syllable

When a syllable ends with a consonant and there is only one vowel in that syllable, the vowel has a short vowel sound.

---

4. Student draws a representation of a cat on notebook and writes the word five times vertically in a column.
   Use the word in a sentence orally.
   Put all materials neatly away.

5. On the second day, student independently builds first word. A second picture is selected and the word is built with help as before.
   Follow the same steps in decoding, labeling the word with word card, writing the word five times in one's notebook and using the word in a sentence.

   Put all materials neatly away.

   Repeat steps with the third word.

6. On the third day, student independently builds first and second words.
   A third picture is selected and the word is built with help as before.
   Follow the same steps in decoding, labeling the word, recording the word in one's notebook and using the word in a sentence.

   Repeat steps with the fourth word on the fourth day.

7. On the fourth day, student builds all four words independently.
   Put all letter cards away.
   Mix four word cards.
   Match word cards to pictures. Compare with check-up card for accuracy.
   Make a story verbally using as many words as you can.

8. With help, decode and learn to read a few words on the additional word list.

Move on to the next set and work on decoding and reading as before.

A table is attached to exemplify sequence in decoding words with short vowels.

WORD READING FLUENCY

Segmenting and blending start out slowly. With practice, decoding improves and what began as a laborious decoding process becomes automatic with quick recall of sounds of letters.

First we build fluency on two-letter words with short vowels, shown below. 45-seconds to complete reading the list is the usual rate. We help by segmenting the word and allowing the student to blend. Students want to check their rate every day and check if they have improved.

am
an
as
at
egg
if
in
is
it
on
ox

up

us

The above word list can be cut up into individual word cards. Take three, four or five cards, practice reading them with the learner. Then ask for one card at a time until all five cards have been handed to the teacher. Line up the cards again and repeat the reading drill process. Rearrange the cards and again ask for each card as before.

Once these words have been read at a reasonable pace, take another set of five cards and read as before. Through practice over a number of times, the slow decoding becomes faster and approaches the speed of reading. What used to sound like a laborious process automatically becomes reading. To give more practice to build fluency, we have grouped words to be read in vertical sequence. We combined the vocabulary used in decoding with the additional word lists to create **families of words**.

The "at" family	The 'ap' family	The 'ad' family
at	cap	dad
fat	map	mad
bat	tap	had
cat	sap	lad
hat	cap	dad
pat	rap	pad
rat	nap	sad
mat	cap	dad
sat		bad
vat		add

The "an" family	The "am" family	The "ag" family
an	am	bag
man	ram	tag
van	dam	sag
pan	ham	rag
ran		gag
can		wag
		lag
		bag

The "as" family
as
has
gas

The "eg" family	The "en" family	The "ell" family
leg	men	bell
peg	ten	tell
beg	hen	sell
egg	wet	fell
yen	vet	well
den	yet	dell
	get	yell
	pet	
	bet	
	set	
	let	

The "ip" family	The "it" family	The "ig" family
lips	kit	pig
tip	fit	wig
zip	mitt	fig
pip	hit	jig
sip	lit	big
dip	bit	
rip	pit	
hip		
nip		

The "in" family	The "id" family	The "ill" family
in	lid	ill
pin	bid	bill
fin	did	hill
bin	hid	mill
tin	kid	pill
win	rid	jill
din		sill
kin		till
		will

The "im" family	The "ib" family
him	bib
rim	rib
kim	nib
tim	
vim	
dim	

The "op" family	The "on" family	The "od" family
pop	on	pod
hop	ton	odd
cop	don	cod
mop	son	nod
top	won	sod
	con	

The "ot" family	The "og" family	The "ob" family
pot	hog	job
hot	dog	bob
cot	log	cob
dot	jog	mob
tot	bog	sob
lot	cog	gob
jot	fog	lob
got		
not		

The "ug" family	The "up" family	The "un" family
mug	up	run
hug	cup	bun
bug	pup	sun
jug	sup	fun
tug		nun
rug		pun
dug		

The "ub" family	The "us" family	The "ut" family
tub	us	nut
sub	bus	cut
cub	fuss	hut
hub		but
rub		gut
sub		

The "um" family	The "ud" family	
gum	bud	
hum	cud	
bum	mud	
sum	dud	
mum		
rum		

The "ack" family	The "eck" family	The "ick" family
tack	neck	pick
sack	deck	sick
pack	peck	tick
rack	heck	kick
lack		wick
		lick

The "ock" family	The "uck" family	
rock	duck	
sock	suck	
dock	tuck	
hock	puck	
lock	luck	
mock	buck	
pock		
cock		

Overall	Our Love of Learning program is a complete, sequential and logical approach to decoding words and being able to read everything. With our method, we imprint relative recall with our proven methodology in a unique and creative way. Beautifully hand illustrated images are combined with word cards, letter card and games to make each level of learning successful for every variety of learning strengths in your classroom Designed for interactive teaching, each card appeals to visual, auditory and touch senses. The lessons engage the mind in creativity and the use of imagination. Welcome to the world of decoding. Welcome to the Love of Learning!
Lesson 1 rhyming (pictures)	Words with the same ending sounds are words that rhyme. This set of 24 colorful 5.5" x 5.5" laminated cards is a fun and effective way of teaching words that rhyme. Use these cards for all types of games!
Lesson 2 Counting number of syllables in a word (pictures)	Syllables are units of pronunciation in a word. With our set of 24 brightly hand drawn 7.5 x 5.5" laminated cards you can teach all units from 1 to 5 syllables!

Lesson 3 Segmenting and blending (pictures)	Breaking up a word into its component vowel and consonant sounds is segmenting. Putting the sounds together to hear a word is blending. We make it easy to teach this component of reading with 8 illustrated 5.5" x 5.5" laminated cards. If you purchase Lessons 1-3 you will begin teaching stepping stones of becoming a word detective!
Lesson 4 Letters of the Alphabet (pictures, colored letters, textured letters)	Each word is composed of letters. Each letter has its own distinct sound. An image of an object which begins with that letter and resembling the shape of the letter is included in this 54 card set of the alphabet. Each 5.5" x 5.5" picture was carefully chosen and matched to the letter it represents. This promotes letter-sound association. Introduce no more than two letters at a time. Avoid teaching any two of these letters (b, d, p, q) together to prevent confusion with left, right or top and bottom orientations of the letters. We suggest teaching these image and letter cards along with the textured cards described below. Our set of 27 7.5" x 5.5" textured letter cards invites the learner to trace the shape of the letter in the same manner that one writes the letter on paper. Each of the letters on these cards is coated with a sandpaper varnish for a tactile experience the child will not forget. This set teaches how one writes with ones fingers without the added difficulty of holding a pencil. These elements of our reading kit are most effective when purchased as a set. They work with each other.

Lesson 5 Words with short vowels a, e, i, o, u, ck (picture cards, individual letters, word cards)	There are five short vowels - **a (as in apple)**, e (as in **egg**), i (as in **inch worm**), o (as in **on**), u (as in **up**). **Our kit contains three sets of lessons for each short vowel and ck. You get 180 beautifully crafted cards in all!** We sound out a word shown by a picture card slowly. We pick out the beginning, middle and final sounds and represent each sound with the letter cards provided to spell the word. Later, we match the spelled word with a single word card. In each of these lessons we provide you 4 carefully selected 5.5" x 5.5" image cards and the corresponding word cards, **but unique to our set of materials** are individual letter cards for word building exercises. We also provide a game card and a solution card and even an additional words card to continue with the lesson far down the road. Cards come to you perforated so you can separate them when you get them.
Lesson 6 Short vowel words with final and initial consonant blends (picture cards, individual letters, word cards)	Two consonants pronounced in succession are called consonant blends. These may appear at the beginning of the word and are called initial blends. Consonant blends may also appear at the end of a word and thus are called final blends. You teach these cards the same way as you teach Lesson 5. There are 36 sets of lessons for each blend in this robust Lesson!

Lesson 7 Long Vowels	All of our booklets are beautifully hand illustrated on 7.5" x 5.5" laminated cards, spiral bound in brightly colored spirals to add joy to your classroom! Each segment of each lesson contains 4 illustrated words and an additional word card to continue lessons well into the future. Thus far, we have only learned the short vowel sounds of a, e, i, o, and u. Each of these letters have long vowel sounds, too. In our Lesson 7 Long Vowel Booklets, you get six 7.5" x 5.5" laminated spiral bound booklets walking you through 127 pages on each of the long vowel sounds. You can easily point with one finger on the single letter saying the long vowel sound and proceed to segment and blend the word as before. Then point with two fingers to the two letter combinations saying the long vowel sound and proceed to segment and blend as before. The booklets are broken into vowels and include the short oo and long oo sounds.
Lesson 8 Consonant Digraphs Book 1	The next step in our lineal program will teach the consonant digraphs. In these two booklets with over 69 pages, we will teach you how to make new sounds with letter combinations. For example, we do not say the sound of "c" nor the sound of "h." Instead we say the new sound of "ch" as in chick. We decode the words in these books using the new digraph we have learned.
Lesson 9 Diphthongs au, aw, oi, oy, ou, ow	Now we move on to our Lesson 9 – Diphthongs. Two vowels pronounced as one syllable is a diphthong. In this 37 page full color illustrated booklet, you point at the new diphthong sound and proceed to decode the word as before.

Lesson 10 r-controlled vowels ar, er, ir, or, ur	The vowels a, e, i, o, u paired with the letter r assume modified sounds as in (ark, fern, bird, corn, fur). Introduce the new sound symbol and proceed to decode the word as before. 31 pages of r-controlled vowels will make it easy and fun to teach this lesson.
Lesson 11 silent e as long vowel marker a...e e...e i...e o...e u...e	The letter e after a consonant modifies the short vowel before the consonant into a long vowel. In this booklet of 31 pages, you will be able to teach this lesson easily and fluidly.
Lesson 12 Other sounds of some consonants ge, gi, gy (j) ci, ce, cy (s) se, sy (z) ed (d), ed(t), ed (ed)	The g in giraffe is pronounced with the j sound. The c in rice has the s sound. The s has the z sound in rose, nose and vase. These are some of the many other sounds that letters make. 61 brightly illustrated pages will walk you through the most common words that do not fall into the norm.

Lesson 13, 14 and 15	We combine our lessons 13, 14 and 15 into one 21 page booklet for you to enjoy. Teach multi- syllable words ending in le, with the sound of l and multi-syllable words ending in y, with the sound of ee. A double consonant after a vowel (h**o**pping) gives that vowel a short vowel sound.
Lesson 16 Silent letters Book 1 silent b (lamb) silent g (sign) silent gh (night) silent h (hour) silent k (knot)	In this 2 booklet lesson, we recognize that some letters in a word are silent. We show you how to proceed to decode the word without voicing the silent letters. 56 pages will guide you through all the silent letters in our vocabulary.

Lesson 17 Exceptions to the Rule	Our set of 6 booklets contain 127 pages of words we normally lump together as Exceptions to the Rules. With our guidelines, we will lead you to discover that even words we classify as exceptions to the rule have rules of their own. This demystifies decoding these words. Instead of casting these words aside as unreadable, we learn new sounds of two-letter combinations (ea as in bread, ea as in break) or the sound of four-letter combinations (tion as in lotion, sion as in mansion) and proceed to decode and blend as before.

Making words longer by joining syllables one could read could be a step towards reading two-, three- or four- syllable words. First read the first syllable, next read the second syllable. Connect the first to the second and you have a **two-syllable word.**

kit-ten	pig- let	bed-bug
mit-ten	bas-ket	win-ner
box-er	rock-et	din-ner
nut-meg	pock-et	dip-per
rib-bon	bet-ter	but-ter
pic-nic	buck-et	zip-per
box-er	nut-meg	cat-nip

Putting two- or three-word phrases together

When children first learned to talk, they spoke one word at a time. It took a few months before the child joined two words together to form a phrase. Following that sequence of development, we now will form two- or three word phrases that the child can read.

Since the student can read all short vowel words, we can make phrases from combining any word from the short a, short e, short i, short o, short u and final ck word lists.

red	cap		big	bed
red	van		red	lips
ten	cups		hot	cup
big	jug		big	mat
hot	mug			

sit	on	a	bed
bug	on	a	rug
man	in	a	van
duck	on	a	rock
tag	on	a	bag
jam	on	a	bun

zip	the	big	bag
fun	in	a	bus
bell	on	a	hill
kick	the	puck	
pod	in	the	pot
sock	in	the	tub

VOCABULARY INSTRUCTION

Reference: National Reading Panel Chapter 4 pp 15-28

Vocabulary is tied to text comprehension. Vocabulary is concerned with only one unit, one word, comprehension is concerned with a bigger number of units. Comprehension is aided by an understanding of what relevant words mean. Likewise, comprehension is blocked when one does not know what a key vocabulary means.

Basically there are two main categories of vocabulary: receptive (listening or reading) and productive (speaking or writing). We have a larger receptive vocabulary than productive vocabulary. It is advisable that we seek to continuously expand our receptive and productive vocabulary. Text comprehension is facilitated with a wider receptive vocabulary. Clarity and specificity of speech is aided with enough variety and expanse of words at one's command.

There are two main avenues for developing vocabulary: **direct** and **indirect.** Direct instruction is planned and structured for the purpose of gaining the meaning of a few selected words. This is usually conducted prior to reading a story or a science lesson. Introducing the new words with their corresponding meanings paves the way to understanding the story or passage in science. This is even more effective when the student is active in the process such as making a sentence using the word or creating an image that makes the word memorable. Repetition of the target word several times increases its acquisition, retention and integration with the learner's vocabulary.

Some methods using **direct instruction** include the following: semantic mapping, using keyword, learner's association of the word with one's own experience, writing the word in one's vocabulary notebook. Word analysis showing root and affixes gives a handle on word's meaning through its etymology.

Indirect method is unplanned as a separate activity. In the course of reading a story or a passage, the learner encounters a new word that makes one pause to ask what the word means. This is a teachable moment. Teacher and learner explore the meaning of the word then read the sentence with the new word and see how the new vocabulary enriches the meaning of the whole sentence.

Other indirect methods include the following: the learner infers the meaning from the context of the story, the word's part of speech. Indirect method is incidental learning, learner extracts the meaning of the word from listening or reading the passage. Mentor can restructure the task so learner can accomplish the task independently. Restructuring may be done by substituting easy words for more difficult ones. A sentence with several dependent clauses may be simplified by eliminating clauses without sacrificing its main story line.

The National Reading Panel recommends that vocabulary needs to be taught directly and indirectly. A combination of methods is more effective than using a single method. Computers and multi-media may be used in facilitating vocabulary learning.

<u>Text Comprehension</u>

Three factors need to be considered in understanding text comprehension:

<u>Vocabulary</u>

<u>Sentence structure or grammar</u>

<u>Type of essay or narrative</u>

Role of vocabulary in text comprehension

The role of vocabulary in text comprehension has been discussed under the subject of vocabulary instruction.

Words in isolation are understood a certain way, when combined with other words in a phrase or a sentence it may mean differently.

The type of sentence (descriptive, imperative, exclamatory) confers its appropriate meaning to the word or words.

The tense (verb) specifies whether an action had taken place, is taking place, will take place or one wishes it to take place.

The function of the word in a sentence is important to recognize.

Who is the doer of the action? (subject)

What was the action? (verb, predicate)

What was the object of the action? (direct object)

To whom was the object directed? (indirect object)

Is the subject of the sentence the doer of the action? If so it is in the active case. If not, it is in the passive case.

Longer sentences have to be analyzed whether there are several independent clauses or there is one main clause with one or more subordinate clauses.

Sentence analysis skills greatly help in understanding the meaning of the sentence. Sentence analysis needs to be integrated with comprehension studies.

CARLOS'S LETTER TO THE STAFF

Carlos came along for the ride with his mom on her way to a staff meeting at the school. He was four years old and had attended Glencoe Montessori School since he was three.

He entertained himself at the office while a staff meeting was going on. Shortly after the meeting started, he came to the meeting and handed four sheets of letterhead paper with some pen writing on them. The note was meant to be read to the staff during the meeting. His note was addressed to the staff.

With his knowledge of phonics up to that point, he managed to write a coherent message reminding the staff to come on time. He then itemized what the staff or teachers should teach the children at the school:

> Teachers hold the hand of infants and help them to walk.

> Toddlers can be helped to build the pink tower.

> Preschoolers can be engaged with practical life activities.

> Kindergartners can study math with the equipment. Teachers need to know math and teach it without a "goof"

What was admirable was the fact that Carlos knew the school curriculum from infancy to kindergarten and the sequence in providing the teaching-learning experiences appropriate for each level.

Carlos knew the basic sounds of the alphabet, some blends and digraphs. He did his best in representing other sounds unfamiliar to him with what he knew.

In the final analysis, Carlos thought of himself as an administrator interested in making the school a place "Where the child is a child." The last phrase was Carlos's contribution to the school brochure when asked for a statement to appear on the brochure.

GLENCOE MONTESSORI SCHOOL
1010 FORESTWAY ROAD
GLENCOE, IL 60022
(312) 835-0188

Metings speches
Techers canot
come Late.
Techers haflt
to do Pra. LIFE
rite. Techer must
Tech kids The way
they were taught,
and do it step
after step.

They must Tech
from Baby to
cindergarten

Then they shoud
yous ther math aewitmen
to Help Them learn
ther math.
day by day a child
learns only if the
Techer Teches
The rite way.

SEVERAL COATS OF PAINT AS APPLIED TO VOCABULARY LEARNING

After applying one coat of paint on the wall, I could only see a faint trace of color from the paint. I was told to allow the paint to dry for a while then come back and apply a second coat. I followed the advice. The second coat covered the surface with the color, smooth and bright. A third coat even made the wall look brighter. It brought the glossy quality of the paint. Each application brought more color and covered the wall with more opacity.

The first coat served as a primer to prepare the surface for the next application. The primer basically served a dual purpose: 1) to penetrate the wood to prepare the surface for the next application and 2) to link up with the new layer of paint to be applied. It takes at least two applications for paint to be effective in covering the surface. We also need to give time for the paint to dry and form the hard surface upon drying as a result of oxidation. The painting process gave me a metaphor for teaching and learning. The first coat or first introduction to the lesson prepares the student for the lesson. This orients the student to what one is about to learn. One is not focused since the subject matter is relatively new. After giving the student time to become familiar with the broad picture of the subject matter, one begins to focus. With repetition and practice and reintroduction in various ways using different modalities of learning style, (visual, auditory, kinesthetic), the new lesson becomes an acquaintance and in time it becomes a friend. That is when mastery of the concept or skill can be demonstrated. The process takes time and varies with each individual student. **Let's apply this to learning vocabulary.**

First application of a coat of paint

Before reading a story or an expository article, select three or four words from the narrative that are significant to the story and most likely would be unfamiliar to the students. For example: From the story "The Quiltmaker's Journey" by Jeff Brumbeau and Gail de Marcken, the first word to be introduced is **quilt** and its derivatives quilting, quilt maker. Show samples of quilt designs on paper. (Visual) Demonstrate how some of the designs are executed by coloring squares or triangles on half-inch squares. (Kinesthetic) Discuss how cloth quilts were first made to piece together scraps of cloth left over from a previous sewing project. The resulting multicolored blanket not only made use of the scrap fabric but also made something that will keep us warm. (Meaning-Function of quilt)

We just learned a new meaningful word that we will meet again in the story. We then spell it with movable alphabet (letter cut-outs) as we sound out the syllable. We write the word on an erase board using red pen for qu and black for **i, l** and **t. {qu i l t}**

Students write the vocabulary word five times in their notebook. Each one orally says a sentence using the word "quilt". Introduce the two other words in like manner

Quilting, the act of making a quilt.

Quilt Maker, one who makes quilts.

The **second word** to be introduced is **journey.** A journey is a long trip. One can travel by sea on boat or ship, by air on an airplane or on land by car or on foot. Find out how the woman in the story travelled. Decide how you are going to make your journey and draw or cut out pictures that go with your journey.

The **third word** is **poverty,** being poor. Some poor people have no homes. They find places to sleep in public places and keep themselves warm with blankets. Students can illustrate this word by drawing either a small house, people sleeping under a tree or other conditions to show poverty, being poor.

The students draw their pictures to illustrate the key vocabulary introduced. The group reassembles after a reasonable time to listen to the story.

Second Application of a Coat of Paint

The teacher first shows the pages of the book without reading the story to get to whet their appetite for the story. The students are encouraged to say what they think the story is all about. A few questions are asked to check background knowledge. (**oral communication**)

Key questions about the events that will be read from the story will be asked to prepare them to anticipate the events. The vocabulary words on individual cards are displayed on the board and **reviewed.**

Third application of the Coat of Paint

After reading the story, the vocabulary words are reviewed and students are asked where in the story did they hear those words. (**review**) Questions to check on comprehension and critical thinking are asked to complete the lesson. (**comprehension, critical thinking**)

Other Suggested Activities

Other activities may be engaged depending on the class. Students may choose their favorite part of the story, read it and tell the class why they like that part.

Students may suggest what they think the moral lesson from the story could be.

Students may retell orally the story in their own way.

The class may dramatize a scene from the story.

A GUIDE TO MENTORING STUDENTS IN LEARNING TO READ

1. Teach students who are ready to learn. Take the ones who are most ready first, the rest may "catch the next train."

2. Everyone is ready to learn something, it is the observer's duty to find out what one is ready for. When one is not ready for a certain lesson, offer the prerequisite lesson or lesson before the target lesson.

3. Make lessons short and interesting.

4. Use the general principle of going from the known to the unknown. Start with what the learner knows to bridge to the new concept to be learned.

5. Movement is a big factor in learning. Use large movements (big arm movements in writing letters on the board, walking, jumping to outline the letter on the ground).

6. Break major skills into its simpler units and master one skill before undertaking the next one. Learn to trace the textured letters with the index and middle fingers. This serves two purposes:
   a) learning to "write" with fingers using the appropriate stroke
   b) to practice the stroke without the added difficulty of holding the pencil and worrying about pencil control.

7. Since the writing-reading process involves manual, auditory and visual skills, involve student in activities that develop these skills in other activities (art and practical life for visual and manual skills, music for auditory skills).

8. Frequent short lessons are more effective than long lessons with long intervals between lessons.

9. Be positive, encouraging and enjoy the lesson.

10. Know the reasons for using the different materials. Letter cards to spell words in the lesson invite movement and eliminate the history of error.

   Textured letters are used to impart the tactile experience in learning. One can feel the texture when one is appropriately tracing the shape of the letter.

   The pictures for each letter in the alphabet chart were chosen to say the initial sound of the letter while resembling the shape of the letter.

11. The order of the letters in the alphabet chart is meant to separate "b" from "d" and "p" to minimize left to right reversals or top to bottom reversals.

12. Each lesson begins with a review, followed by a new lesson. A reinforcement activity follows after the lesson to give learner time to reflect and seal the lesson in one's memory.

13. Language involves speaking and listening as well as reading and writing. Interaction in meaningful conversation is necessary and is helpful in making informal assessments.

14. When learner is ready to read, follow these three steps:
   a) read to the student

      b) read with the student

      c) let student read to you

15. There is a time lag from the teaching time to the time student shows new learning. Be patient. Continue to teach, adjusting pace, content and type of activity. Nothing is lost. In due time, all teaching efforts will be rewarded.

16. When a group of students is ready to read, read to the group the same book for at least four days. Allow students to read along especially at some repetitive verses.

17. Allow a student to read along commercially prepared books or one you recorded yourself. When student can read one book independently, record the student and send the tape or CD home.

BIBLIOGRAPHY

01) Addyman, Caspar, 2017 Mothers Adopt a Universal Tone of Voice When They Talk To <u>Babies</u> : <u>https://www.smithsonianmag.com</u>

02) Armstrong, Thomas, 2003. <u>The multiple intelligences of reading and writing.</u> ASCD Association for supervision and curriculum development, Alexandria, Virginia.

03) Center for Disease Control and Prevention www.cdc.gov/ActEarly |1-800-CDC-INFO (1-800-232-4636)

04) Chomsky, Noam, 1977. <u>On Language</u>. The New Press, New York, 2007.

05) Crystal, David, 2012. <u>*Spell it out.*</u> St. Martin's Press. New York, N.Y.

06) Darwin, Charles, 2005. Darwin: The indelible stamp, The evolution of an idea Edited and commentary by James Watson. Running Press, Philadelphia * London. <u>Book 1 The Voyage of the Beagle.</u> Pages 3 - 337

07) Darwin, Charles, 2005. Darwin: The indelible stamp, The evolution of an idea Edited and commentary by James Watson. Running Press, Philadelphia * London. <u>Book 3 The Descent of Man and Selection in Relation to Sex</u> pages 607 – 1059

08) Flesch, Rudolf (1965). Why Johnny Can't Read and what you can do about it.

09) Gardner, Howard, 1983, 2004, 2011. <u>Frames of mind</u>: the theory of multiple intelligences. Basic books, New York.

10) Harcourt-Smith, W.E.H. and L C Aiello, "Fossils, feet and the evolution of human bipedal locomotion," J. Anat May, 2004 204 (5); 403-416

11) Kenneally, Christine "What makes language distinctly human: talking through time." Scientific American September, 2018 pp.55-59.

12) Laland, Steven "How we became a different kind of animal," Scientific American September 2018 pp.33-39

13) Lyon, G. Reid 1998. Why Reading Is Not a Natural Process. Educational Leadership February 1998

14) Medary, Marjorie, 1954. *Each one teach one. Frank Laubach, friend to millions.* Longmans, Green and Co. New York, London, Toronto.

15) Montessori, Maria, 1964. The Montessori Method. Schoken Books, New York.

16) NAEYC position statement: Overview of learning to read and write: developmentally appropriate practices for young children. Adopted May, 1998.

17) Chomsky, Noam and Piaget, Jean debate (1980). Language and Learning. Edited by Massimo Piateli, Harvard University Press, Cambridge, Massachusetts.

18) Pinker, Steven, The Language Instinct: How the mind creates language. (1994). Harper Collins Publishers Inc. New York, N

19) United States. National Commission on Excellence in Education. (1983). *A nation at risk : the imperative for educational reform : a report to the Nation and the Secretary of Education, United States Department of Education. Washington, D.C.: The Commission: [Supt. of Docs., U.S. G.P.O. distributor],* Reading Excellence Act February, 2000 National Reading Panel Report Chapter 4 Comprehension, Vocabulary Instruction

20) Wong, Kate. "Lucy's baby: evolution upright walking." Scientific American Dec., 2006 pp. 78-85.

21) Wong, Kate. "The human saga: evolution rewritten." Scientific American Sept, 2014 pp. 36-39.

22) Zender, Marc Writing and Civilization: From Ancient Worlds to Modernity. The Great Courses.